Reading
the Clouds

Reading *the* Clouds

MISSION SPIRITUALITY
for
NEW TIMES

Anthony J. Gittins

Liguori
LIGUORI, MISSOURI

Published by Liguori Publications
Liguori, Missouri
http://www.liguori.org

Library of Congress Cataloging-in-Publication Data

Gittins, Anthony J.
    Reading the clouds : mission spirituality for new times / Anthony J. Gittins. —1st ed.
        p. cm.
    Includes bibliographical references.
    ISBN 0-7648-0499-5 (pb)
    1. Missions—Theory. 2. Spirituality—Catholic Church. I. Title.
BV2063.G53   1999
253—dc21   99–23344

Printed in the United States of America
03 02 01 00 99   5 4 3 2 1
First Edition

The world is charged with the grandeur of God
GERARD MANLEY HOPKINS

Nothing endures but change
HERACLITUS

"*When you see a cloud rising in the west, you immediately say,*
'It is going to rain'; and so it happens. And when you see the
south wind blowing, you say, 'There will be scorching heat'; and
it happens. You hypocrites! You know how to interpret the
appearance of earth and sky, but why do you not know how
to interpret the present time?"
LUKE 12:54–56

Contents

Foreword

Reading the Clouds

K iribati is a nation whose islands are scattered like loose pearls across the Pacific. Here the International Date Line meets the equator. Between the main island of Tarawa and its neighbor Maiana, there lies a deceptively short reach of ocean. But it is possible to set sail and leave Tarawa behind an hour or more before sighting Maiana.

For city slicker or landlubber, the open sea is an awesome place with power to inspire emotions as varied as the weather and the shape of the waters. The pleasure experienced in the tranquillity of an ocean-going liner on a blessed windless day is simply not to be compared to the sheer exhilaration to be found in a fragile boat riding the troughs and swells miles from land.

Three of us sat in the fourteen-footer with its small outboard motor. Out of sight of land and alternately plunged into deep troughs and suspended high on the crest of a swell, we were caught between the immensity of sea and sky as we rode the deepest, blackest-velvet waters on earth. If the experience has become more truly awesome in retrospect, at the time it was simply spell-binding!

One of the navigators pointed to where sea and sky met. "Look!" he cried, excitedly. Though I saw nothing, my camera aimed and clicked. Five minutes later he motioned again: "See!" Still nothing, but again I snapped the camera shutter. Only then could I begin to make out a smudge, a wisp of something dancing above and beyond the horizon, far, far away. "Fish!" proclaimed the navigator, adding confusion to my ignorance. Not *flying* fish, surely, I thought! Yet within moments I could identify thousands upon thousands of diving, swooping birds. And then we were among them. The air was black with birds. The screams and the beat of wings were deafening.

The second sailor was by now pulling his fishing line from the ebony waters as often and as fast as he could—no bait, simply a colored plastic lure—an iridescent yellow-fin tuna, bigger than a forearm, soon covered the boat's planking. The harvest was abundant though the laborers were few. But the two of them had the eyes to see what neither my eyes nor my camera's sharp lens had captured. They had seen the birds, far from land, and they knew the meaning. For to fish well and navigate well, one must also be a good interpreter.

Birds whose natural habitat is a Pacific island live on fish. They do not routinely fly off across the uncharted ocean, but they do go in search of their food. That day on the lonely immensity of the Pacific, I learned some very useful lessons, from and about nature.

First: to the trained observer's eye, to *see* birds is to *perceive* fish, for where birds are above there are fish beneath—the birds are "spotting" the shoal. Thus, to fish well, one must have good eyes first for the birds. Not surprisingly, the mariners' eyes are well trained, and over many years they develop prodigious vision. With their amazing visual ability they see much better than bespectacled eyes and self-focusing camera combined! (The first two photographs taken minutes after the navigator pointed to the birds show no trace of their presence.) Moreover, sailors' sight becomes instrumental in their heightened perception. For a mariner, lack of sight is lack of perception. And without *perception,* what is invisible will simply remain uninterpreted. But first, one must know where to look, and for what.

The second lesson is more subtle: where there are birds, land is not far away. Huge flocks of birds go fishing, gorge themselves, and return to their natural habitat. Low-flying birds are an indication, not of seasonal migration but of routine activity. A mariner on the open ocean who sees birds not only perceives the chance of good fishing but the proximity of land, fresh water, and all attendant blessings!

How will the sailor in search of land manage when the telltale birds are absent? This is the third lesson. The mariner's eyes are constantly moving as he "reads" the waters, gleaning vast amounts of information. Many Pacific languages contain a whole repertoire of words for kinds of water—words that mark flow and eddy, drift, current, wave-height, and numerous shades of meaning. Water is never simply generic, but always comes in specific forms, each of which must be interpreted if the mariners are to survive and arrive at their destination. Not surprisingly, the peoples of the Pacific are some of the finest sailors on the face of the globe, with vast knowledge of the seas. Their expertise is recruited avidly by the merchant navies of the world.

The water is not all the sailors read. These argonauts of the Pacific are equally fluent in the language of the sky: the clouds by day and the stars by night. And as we neared the island of Maiana I was given a beginner's lesson in reading the clouds. My desk was the little boat, and the classroom was the vast expanse around and above us. The teacher held the rudder in one hand and pointed to sky and horizon with the other. Land, he explained, breathes oxygen, and the breath rises as cloud. On a windless day the cloud will hardly drift at all. It marks the land which lies beneath it, as clearly as would a flag. But clouds do much more than indicate the presence of land. They may actually reflect it. A trained eye will see blues or yellows or greens on the underside of the clouds, reflecting, in turn, a lagoon, a sandy beach, or a grove of coconuts.

Unless you can read the clouds, you have no business going to sea alone. The mariner who said, "Watch!" was echoing Jesus, who also cautioned his followers to be alert, to stay on watch, in order to see, perceive, and understand.

————

This book is about our common task: the task of interpreting our way through life. Most of us could not hope to acquire the skills needed by Pacific mariners, yet each of us is constantly interpreting the particular worlds in which we live. Or perhaps not. A characteristic malaise of our day is that our senses have become dulled and our interpretive skills are neglected. Often we simply do not perceive. We have eyes but we fail to use them for developing perception and insight. So we do not understand or grow in wisdom through informed meditation on the world around us. Jesus was very concerned about this.

Perhaps, therefore, we should learn to pay more attention: to certain persons and to certain things, whether prosaic or poetic; to the meaning for our lives, of places and times; to the significance of our changing selves; to the importance of people we have encountered; to the gatherings of birds; to the language of clouds.

For centuries, navigators from the Pacific have been committed to reading the clouds as they ride the seas in search of fish and landfall. They can set sail in open boats, travel by day and by night for weeks on end over the trackless ocean and find a piece of land no more than a meter in height and less than a quarter-mile across. And all this without sextant or compass or the instruments of scientific cultures. By contrast, in 1620 the Pilgrims who landed at Provincetown on Cape Cod, Massachusetts, had sailed from England with the benefit of the scientific instruments of their day. They were headed for a continental coastline studded with high mountains, extending from the Arctic to the tropics. It was just as well the target was so large, for they landed six hundred miles from their destination of Jamestown, Virginia!

Latter-day pilgrims, we may need to focus our energies and strengthen our commitment if we are to adequately read the clouds which accompany us on our journeys, and safely reach our final destination.

Introduction

Spirituality, Culture, and a World of Change

This is a book about spirituality. *Another* book about spirituality. So a word of explanation may help get us started. The emphasis here will be on a very down-to-earth spirituality or *way of being in the world with God*. We will try to take seriously both the world—or worlds—we inhabit, and the God who sustains the universe and ourselves. Of course, we cannot neglect the fact that we are embodied as human persons, in all our variety and with our very different experiences. We grow and age, wax and wane, fall and rise, respond and persevere. These are features of who we are; they must be part of our developing spirituality. And since there may be many years, many decades, between our first conscious response to God and our final breath, we also need a spirituality for the long haul, something that will help sustain us.

A central theme will be healing. This focus has become rather fashionable, and it characterizes a certain type of New Age spirituality. That is *not* the reason we will look at healing, but rather because it is at the very heart of the life's work of Jesus. To many of his contemporaries Jesus was first and foremost a healer. Mark's

Gospel tells us that as soon as Jesus stepped ashore at Gennesaret, "people at once recognized him....And all who touched [him] were healed" (6:54, 56).

Another fashionable idea is that we are *wounded healers*. It is true that we are wounded. It is also true that Jesus offers to heal us if we reach out to him for that grace. But that would make us *healed healers*: a rather different story. *Healed* healers have a greater responsibility to be engaged with spreading the good news and extending the healing they themselves have received. *Wounded* healers may connote a little too much self-pity. In this book, could we consider ourselves not just as wounded but also as *healed* healers? As such, we have a mandate that calls for urgent action: to be instruments of outreach and inclusion, healing and reconciliation, ministry and mission.

This book is addressed to all who share a common baptism. Jesus began his public life in the synagogue at Nazareth, where he read from the prophet Isaiah: "The Spirit of the LORD is upon me" (Lk 4:18). On that very basis he constructed his mission and ministry. We have been baptized *by the same Spirit*, and on that basis we should construct the mission and ministry that we undertake as disciples and companions of Jesus. There is room for difference and variety in the Christian community, but we are all one in Christ (1 Cor 12:4–30). Without denying differences among people, we will seek in the following pages to identify some common elements that characterize a spirituality for contemporary Christians in a world at the dawn of a new millennium.

There are two parts: *Part One* looks at what we mean by the call or vocation of each and every believer. *Chapter One* tries to place the call against the background of the broader Jewish-Christian tradition and to show how it is foundational to our identity as believers. *Chapter Two* then asks how we might respond to the call, arguing that the appropriate Christian response is *missionary* in nature.

In *Part Two* the aim is to address some components of a contemporary Christian spirituality as well as to point to how they might be integrated. *Chapter Three* suggests that our cultural and social identities are rooted in shared stories. Stories contain our tribal wisdom or tribal memory, so to speak. If we remember who we are and how we became God's people, we will be able to undertake our Christian responsibilities to the wider community, as healed healers. If we forget our stories we will forget who we are; and without a strong identity we will be unable to act as the *People of God.*

Chapter Four continues the theme of ministry as healing outreach; and in *Chapter Five* we develop two further, and related, points. First, we see how our tradition shows us why and how healing is intrinsic to ministry. Second, we identify the prophetic challenge at the heart of the Jewish-Christian tradition. If we take our faith, our call, and our response seriously, we must face up to our own *prophetic* responsibility.

The final chapters address the topics of incarnation and change. *Chapter Six* starts from the fact that Christianity is the religion of incarnation, embodiment, humanness. Jesus came among us, not as angel or spirit but as a male human being. His ministry was undertaken with that perspective and that limitation. We consider what this might entail for us, whether male or female, as being incarnated or embodied in a rich variety of ways. *Chapter Seven* then takes up the question of change: we live in changing times, and our spirits are housed in changing bodies. What does this imply for our spirituality? How does it affect the way we minister? What difference does it make if we are young or old, healthy or sick?

And so we conclude. Only selected topics will be raised, but one particular perspective will be privileged in these pages. That is the perspective of the Christian who is consciously on the move: not rushing around (much less in circles!), but moving from his or her own center of gravity or comfort zone, to the edges or margins or boundaries, whether they mark neighborhoods or national borders. The Christian is one who follows Jesus, who is the Way, the Truth, and the Life. The earliest Christians were called "Followers of the Way." The assumption underlying this book is that we, too, are, and will always be, to some extent "on the way," *en route*, because we remain followers of the one who never stopped moving to encounter others in love, reconciliation, and healing.

Reading
the Clouds

Part One

———

THE
IDEA
OF A
CHRISTIAN
VOCATION

Chapter One

From Call to Response

The faith that moves mountains counts on the impossible and knows how to read the signs of the times that announce the possibility of a new tune instead of the old refrain.

EBOUSSI BOULAGA

We sanitize Jesus. We blunt his sharp edge. We admire him but we do not follow him.

JESSE JACKSON

The parish community, as the real expression of a local church, cannot limit its attention to the search for justice and intimacy among its members; it must be prepared to take up the cross, standing against evil and injustice wherever they exist in the world.

NATHAN MITCHELL

The Search for Meaning

"Curiosity is one of the permanent and certain characteristics of a vigorous mind," said Samuel Johnson, maker of dictionaries and coiner of aphorisms. Sooner or later, curiosity leads to puzzlement, which appears to be a universal human experience. If nothing puzzles us anymore, we have probably lost our curiosity, our appetite for life.

Not only are personal experiences sometimes baffling, but the world itself can appear as an enigma. The sheer range of cultures worldwide confirms that people *make* meaning rather than simply discover it, for meaning varies with environment and social context. Interpretation of the world, and the production of shared meanings, are tasks that face every society and every person within society.

Jesus was distressed at meeting people who were perfectly able to agree on the various meanings of sky or wind but who seemed quite unpuzzled by—and even unaware of—the meanings of other and more pertinent events: the signs of the times. He warned them sternly to attend to the critical issues and not to dissipate their energies on less important things (Lk 12:54–56). It is a warning his followers have tried to remember.

We Christians are on pilgrimage, committed to a journey yet without knowing quite where it will lead; committed to a process yet with no clear view of the result. But we do not simply float on the prevailing currents from baptism to burial. The voyage demands attentiveness to the Spirit who leads, not only in dramatic ways but also more subtly, and whose inspirations appear to come from many directions over the course of a lifetime.

How are we to remain attentive to this Spirit without losing our sense of responsibility and direction? How can we keep our focus without becoming myopic or mesmerized? This delicate task becomes more complex and taxing because our circumstances—our lives, and the daily needs and challenges—are unfolding in unpredictable ways. How many of us can look back even five years and say that we knew then where we would be now? How many have made careful plans with mature stewardship, only to encounter events which no one could have foreseen?

Chaos Theory warns us that everything, however insignificant, produces a kind of ripple effect that helps to create the future; it tells us that where we are at this moment is the outcome of a whole series of previous events. If we believe God created out of chaos, forming and giving meaning to creation, then should we not seek traces of this creativity in the contemporary world? Jesus constantly assured his followers that God, too, is a creative meaning-maker, and that those who trust in Providence have the possibility of interpreting the world. He taught his disciples in words like these:

"Do not worry, saying, 'What will we eat?' or 'What will we drink?' or 'What will we wear?' For it is the Gentiles who strive for all these things; and indeed your heavenly Creator knows that you need all these things. But strive first for the reign of God and God's righteousness, and all these things will be given to you as well. So do not worry about tomorrow, for tomorrow will bring worries of its own" (Mt 6:25–34).

How might we blunt the criticism which Jesus leveled against those whose curiosity was dulled and who failed to read and interpret the signs of the times? How can we be flexible yet principled, spontaneous yet responsible, risktakers and yet not imprudent? The Christian pilgrimage will take us through difficult territory. Perhaps we can identify some of the components of an informal *theology of call,* by considering the competing demands of the initiative-taker and the true follower or disciple of Jesus. This chapter is an invitation to ponder the call that is an intrinsic part of the baptism that unites Christians to one another and to Christ.

Called to Become

In the winter of 1947, the pride of the London Zoo was a huge, beautiful, white bear. Yet it was lonely, for its mother was dead and it had never known its father. Far from polar ice and snow and vast empty spaces, it only knew the temperate weather of England and the thousands of curious visitors.

During an unusually cold snap, the small lake within the bear's enclosure froze. The ice, though two or three inches thick, was not safe to walk on. At the edge of the lake the bear tapped the ice with its enormous paw, the ice cracked, and the bear took a deep, contented dive. But the huge animal never surfaced. Strangely, it died beneath the ice—not from a sudden heart attack or stroke, but by drowning! Totally unaccustomed to ice above its head, the polar bear had apparently panicked and been unable to locate the original ice hole. It certainly had the power to crack the ice, but it lacked the experience and the memory. And so it drowned. It had not so much forgotten, but perhaps had never really known, what it was to be a polar bear!

It is not only polar bears who forget, or never really know who they are. Many of us behave in the same way. And some of us fail to update or reassess our changing identity. So we do not grow up, we do not act our age, or we become old before our time. Jesus constantly tried to encourage people to know and truly own who they were: beloved children of God. Despite their lack of experience as God's children, and despite an operative theology which belittled many of them or treated them as outcasts, they found themselves affirmed by the Nazarene who welcomed everyone he met, and who was committed to exposing the lie that God had favorites or that some people were beyond redemption. The ministry of Jesus was inclusive, never exclusive. His call was to each and to all. His forgiveness and reconciliation were without limit.

So much for two millennia ago. Can we say that we ourselves experience God's call in our own lives? What is the place of the biblical tradition in our discernment or testing of a call? The language of *call* or *vocation* is not unfamiliar to us. But there was a time when these words were applied exclusively to clergy and religious. Today, we are much more aware that *every* baptized person is called in a special fashion. Yet sometimes we forget, and fail to live up to, the implications of that notion. So perhaps we should pause and reexamine the nature of this call. Not only is that important in itself, but its implications are enormous. We will consider some of them in the next chapter. Meanwhile, the call may be identified in terms of its *persistence*, its *clarity*, and its *concreteness*.

First, persistence. God's call is not static, fleeting, once and for all, or easily missed. God does not try to trick us with a call so subtle that we might not notice it. God loves us more than we love ourselves. Characteristically in the Jewish and Christian traditions, the call is repeated, insistent, and varied.

A classic example is the call of God's Spirit to Elijah, and the whole story is worth rereading (1 Kgs 18:20—19:18). After escaping from Jezebel and running for his life, Elijah was deep in the trackless wilderness and so afraid that he wished he were dead. Touched by an angel, he was sufficiently encouraged to walk for forty days and forty nights in response to the God who called him. Finally, he stood on the holy mountain, waiting....

Yahweh passed by, so the biblical text tells us. First there was a mighty, rock-shattering wind; but God was not in the wind. Then followed an earthquake; but God was not in the earthquake. Next there was a fire; but Yahweh was not in the fire. Three dramatic, cataclysmic natural phenomena occurred, at precisely the time Elijah was looking for a sign. Yet God was not to be found in any of these. Finally, as we recall, there was the whisper of a gentle breeze; and God's equally gentle voice, now distinctly audible, ordered Elijah to return the way he had come, and anoint those who would be pointed out to him.

The experience of Elijah was in the form of an unfolding process rather than as a simple event. So, too, we may become aware of the gentle voice of God as it touches our consciousness like soft music awakening us from sleep; it did not begin only when we became aware of it, but had been in the air for some time. And just as God's call may impinge on our awareness gradually, so our response may take a whole lifetime.

Second, clarity. A call is discerned as authentic not simply if it is unequivocal, much less, pleasant or convenient. Jeremiah wanted to demur: "Ah, Lord God; look, I do not know how to speak, for I am only a boy!" (Jer 1:6ff). Jonah was quite rude: The word of Yahweh was addressed to Jonah: "Up!" he said. "Go at once to Nineveh." …Jonah decided to run away from Yahweh and to go to Tarshish (Jon 1:1–3). Isaiah's response when he saw God was: "Woe is me! I am lost, for I am a man of unclean lips." But a seraph flew down from God's throne and touched his mouth with a live coal, saying: "Now that this has touched your lips, your guilt has departed and your sin is blotted out"(Isa 6:5–7). No more excuses for Isaiah! Or think of Mary the mother of Jesus, the Samaritan woman at the well, and many other characters depicted in biblical stories who were not absolutely sure about the nature or the implications of the call. Certainly it was not always easy: but it was very clear.

It is those who hear the word of God and put it into practice (Mt 7:24) who are true disciples, not those who profess their obedience and then do exactly what they want (Mt 21:28–32). A *fiat* is a faith-response, not a contract. It is a response to a call, and is not simply a whim. Since God is pledged to a covenantal relationship with each of us—a binding agreement never to abandon us (Deut 4:31; Isa 49:15)—we can expect confirmation, a sign, or some endorsement. As we learn the stories of our forebears in the faith, we encounter such indications of God's abiding presence. What we do know if we ponder these stories is that God's call invites to a *transformative* response, a response that taps into our deepest and perhaps unknown qualities. Those who keep a strict tally of their gifts and resources are unlikely to rise to the demands of God's call.

Third, concreteness is a characteristic of the call. God's call, though perfectly real, might never be captured on a tape recorder, and though quite loud to the inner ear it might be inaudible to our closest neighbor. Sometimes when we take an initiative, we imagine we are actually responding to a call. But an initiative is quite different. An initiative is a first step or originating move, unprompted, and consciously self-generated. A call by contrast originates outside the individual, is a kind of prompting, and invites a response. A call implies some form of relationship, and in the Christian tradition at least it implies mutuality.

God's Idea of a Covenant

It is quite remarkable that we routinely assume we can have a relationship with God: a developing, transforming, sustaining relationship. This is perhaps the greatest novelty a Jewish-Christian understanding of God contributes to people of other religious worlds. The simple *fact* that God exists may not be problematic for such people. *Where* God exists may be evident to them in nature and from experience. But the idea that God—Creator, transcendent, perhaps immanent in creation—should entertain a personal, individual, intimate engagement with human beings is often too preposterous for them to contemplate. Yet for those with common Abrahamic religious roots (Jews, Christians, Muslims), it is the basis of our faith, and our covenantal heritage. For Christians, it is also—and particularly—the keystone of the Incarnation. As a special characteristic of the Christian tradition, this astounding notion should never be taken for granted. The success of our Christian response is measured by the seriousness with which we attend to this amazing relationship, expressed so memorably for us in the story of Abraham who left his land *because he knew the call*. Joan Chittister puts it beautifully.

Because Abraham was attuned to the voice of God, he survived what would have been impossible for him to withstand otherwise. Abraham's journey fails over and over...But Abraham feels no defeat...Because he has talked to God, because God has talked to him, only the voice of God itself is the measure of his meaning and his success (Chittister, 1995:49).

The gospels show how Jesus called people, irrespective of social status. Sadly, two thousand years' experience demonstrates just as clearly that such an inclusive welcome has not always been a hallmark of believers. Sometimes other people's identity and social context have been demeaned or repudiated by Christians. Sometimes considerable effort and even violence have been expended in the name of Jesus Christ, in order to uproot and change other people. Though Jesus was clearly committed to the transformation of individuals and of society, and though he always challenged them to conversion of life, he always encountered them *as they were* and *where they were*. He knew that only when someone is taken seriously, as a subject of a relationship and not as an object, can that person experience transformation leading to transcendence. Jesus always treated people as subjects. He invited, challenged, evoked a response, called people to move from where they were and who they were, to where they were called to be and who they were called to become. The same applies to our own call and response.

To leave where we are and to go where we choose: is this a response to a call? Foxes have lairs, but Jesus had nowhere to lay his head; he went from place to place, as he said, "for that is what I came to do" (Mk 1:38); and he reminded Peter that people would lead him where he did not *choose* to go (Jn 21:18). The distinction between a response and an initiative is important. Can we assume our own commitment to preserving the distinction and to discerning God's call in our lives? Can we further assume we do not take our developing relationship with God lightly, but are aware that it is reciprocal or mutual—even though unequal—as well as covenantal? ("You will be my people, and I will be your God," occurs five times in the Bible: Ex 6:7; Jer 7:23; 11:4; 30:22; Ez 36:28). How, then, might we actually identify God's call to us, concretely, existentially, *as we are* and *where we are*?

What does it even mean to say that God calls us as we are? Who are we really? It is a tremendously difficult question to answer. As long as there have been people there have been attempts to solve this particular puzzle. Without doubt, human curiosity has produced some great religious wisdom. Part of the answer can be found by personal introspection. Another part can be sought in dialogue, which requires a broader social context. We can tap both these sources, each fed by revelation and tradition and by the conviction of God's own participation in our private and social conversations. But if God really calls us as we are, and engages with who we are, then God must somehow acknowledge not only our common humanity but the differences between us, our individual uniqueness: the implications are enormous.

Called to Conversion

Carl Jung maintained that conversion is for the second half of life, when we really begin to absorb the implications of our mortality. Until that realization we are not yet aware or wise enough for conversion. Likewise, conductor Seiji Ozawa says, "Mahler's music is like life: you cannot conduct it when you're young. You need to be older to understand life and to conduct Mahler—at least to have a credible relationship with it."

We are changing. For many of us, understanding this fact is like witnessing a breaking dawn. It is not just that we *have* changed but that change marks our lived experience: it is part of who we are. Our bodies wax and wane. We become sick and sometimes we recover. But we become aware that we are mortal. Our "selves" are not immutable.

We are not perfect. As we age and perhaps gain further insights into our real selves and into the gap between who we wanted to be and who we actually are, we may acknowledge addictions, failures, sinfulness. Perhaps, too, we may perceive this fact: that the call is not *literally* to "be perfect as your Heavenly Father is perfect"—as if we were God—but to be "perfected" or made more whole and wholesome, and filled with integrity, just as God is characterized by integrity. We must strive, of course, yet we must also acknowledge our finiteness, our need of redemption, along with our perfectibility. That is also part of who we are.

And we are certainly not infallible. Our lives are littered with mistakes, some serious. Often we have been downright wrong. Sometimes we have changed our minds and repented, returned home like a prodigal child. The older we get the more we may acknowledge our erring ways, or the temptation to deny our mistakes and to try, pathetically, to cover our tracks. That, too, is part of who we are.

So when, perhaps, after four or five decades of living, we are finally struck by the realization that death is approaching and we are still not perfect and still quite capable of failure, then we might be more responsive to that call from God that never really went away. Then we might turn back and discover the promise of a relationship with God, who accepts us unconditionally. But first we must realize, experientially, that we cannot control everything. It's a lesson Peter learned when he, a competent professional fisherman, went fishing and failed to catch a thing (Jn 21:3ff). Finally he listened to the call, cast his nets where he would never have chosen, and was overwhelmed by fish!

Called As Community

A further question: where are we? We do not exist outside a context and thus God does not call us in a vacuum. The call is in the concreteness of the here and now. We should pay close attention to where we are, for all around there are agents and instruments and channels of God's call. Typical, though not always acknowledged, are these four potential channels: a community, a companion or soul-friend, a major personal transition or trauma, and a radicalization of a longstanding commitment.

First, for all of us, the Jewish-Christian story of God is played out in the context of community. God calls *a people*: individuals are called from or to a community, and perhaps both. God is experienced in a social context. We must not privatize our relationship with God and ignore other people or demean God's creation, for *everything* God created was good. All of it. If the Incarnation means anything, it is surely that God in Jesus demonstrates that relatedness and community are essential for human and godly living. Saint Paul develops the theme in that splendid passage in First Corinthians where he describes the Christian community. He speaks of many gifts scattered prodigally among the members of the community by "one and the same Spirit, who allots to each one individually just as the Spirit chooses" (12:11). He says, "Now you are the body of Christ and individually members of it" (12:27). It should not surprise us then, that another person, with a different gift than our own, might be an instrument through which God's call may reach us: we are, after all, members of one community. What may surprise us is just how unlikely and unexpected that person might be.

Second, by its resonance with our own deepest intuitions or perhaps because it is so strikingly different from our own, the experience of another person might touch us deeply: it may be truly a vehicle of God's call. Someone may profoundly impress us with the integrity of a life well-lived, a life that appeals to the idealist in us. Such a person may embody for us the possibility of a life of true service, of faith and covenant. Such a one may be an agent for our own call.

Perhaps, by contrast, the life of someone we know may stand as a silent indictment of our own shallowness or selfishness, forcing us to acknowledge something in ourselves that we would never otherwise have known. This is one way, so faith tells us, that God's gentle and insistent call may reach us.

A growing number of people appear to be explicitly discerning God's call in their lives. They are thoroughly dissatisfied with being nominal Christians, and feel distinctly awkward with their personal comfort and status in a world marked by discomfort and deprivation. They are searching for a deeper meaning for their lives and for a greater challenge than the privatized American Dream. They want to believe that God does indeed call, and that there truly is a faith-response which can give added meaning to their lives. Although some appear to discover a kind of "homecoming," through which they realize that what they have been searching for is almost on their doorstep, others have a different experience. They discover that they have long been resisting a commitment that felt distinctly uncomfortable, demanding, unprofitable, or even ridiculous. But then their criteria somehow change, and now that same commitment magnetizes them. Quite often, the catalyst is in the form of a challenge from another person, perhaps a spiritual director or soul-friend (Leech, 1977), and they discover that as their resistance has gradually been whittled away, so they can identify the call as of God. This can be liberating, truly awesome, and a life-enhancing experience.

A third channel may be the impact of a major transition in life: a "midlife crisis," a serious illness, whether physical or mental, the death of a loved one, or perhaps coming to terms with an addiction. There are many such experiences, and each one focuses our attention on life's fundamentals in a way that routine life does not. This might be what has been called *radical disjunction*, a dramatic break(down) in our "normal" life. It is, classically, a catalyst for conversion, a way for God's call to be heard in our lives.

And, finally, perhaps in the quiet of a retreat, or dramatically in the experience of nature's pyrotechnics—a splendid dawn, an awesome hurricane, a cataclysmic earthquake or volcanic eruption, the stillness of a mountaintop—we may be inspired to recommit to our current relationship with God and humanity, so as to radicalize our longstanding commitment and make the past seem monochrome and pallid by comparison. This has been called *radical continuity*. Less dramatic than radical disjunction, it may be more common and is certainly as authentic (Bynum, 1992:27–51). But the authenticity of any conversion is determined by its *radical* nature. It reaches and renews the *roots* of our lives, and is thus a profound experience. Whatever may trigger such radical continuity may therefore be identified by the person of faith as part of God's call.

In summary, God's call is God's gift to us. We encounter it in the actual experience of our lives. We need to accept it, for it is a gift of life. Although it is a particular gift, it is offered to us not simply for our own sake or privately, but for the sake of the community. The reason we are called is in order to be sent. However, more and more of us do not remain in one place for many years, let alone a lifetime. The rate of change in our lives may be quite brisk. This should be taken very seriously as we try to discern how and where God's dynamic call continues to reach us throughout our changing lives.

From Call to Response: The Book of Acts

In the ministry of Jesus, a gathering movement precedes the commissioning: "come" precedes "go." It would be foolhardy then, if not arrogant, were we to presume to go forward without first being called and sent. True, there is a sending forth of every Christian, for everyone is subject to the judgment in chapter 25 of Matthew's Gospel. There we are reminded, in no uncertain terms, that those who claim discipleship are called and sent to reach out, encounter, and respond to the hungry, the thirsty, the stranger, and the naked, the sick or imprisoned: in a word, the needy. Yet the danger of taking an inappropriate and self-serving initiative is ever-present among those whose cultures promote rugged individualism and well-intentioned condescension.

John the Baptizer promised that Jesus would baptize with the Holy Spirit (Mk 1:8). But even Jesus had first to receive what he would subsequently give (Mk 1:10–11). Later, before saying to his followers, "I send you," Jesus would say, *"as the Father has sent me."* In a similar fashion, "as I have loved you" preceded "love one another"; and "as I have done" came before "so you must do." The sequence is invariable; it is important that we reflect on it.

The Acts of the Apostles demonstrates the movement wonderfully well: "What does the Spirit have in mind?" is more to the point than "what do I/we want?" Acts is largely about the Holy Spirit, the chief initiator and promoter of mission and ministry. Where the community's aspirations match the impulses of the Spirit, grace abounds and God's reign is advanced. But sometimes the disciples get carried away. Here are a handful of illustrations which strikingly demonstrate the priority of the *Spirit,* without whom we will surely fail.

- A delegation representing the whole church is sent to Antioch (Acts 15:12), with an accompanying letter admitting that apostolic zeal has sometimes been pastorally inappropriate: "We have heard that certain persons who have gone out from us, though with no instructions from us…have said things to disturb you and have unsettled your minds" (15:24). After an apology there is a striking clarification of pastoral policy: "It has seemed good *to the Holy Spirit and to us* to impose on you no further burden than these essentials" (15:28). This represents the standard, official approach, reiterated throughout Acts: discernment of what God's Spirit has in mind [call], followed by compliance with whatever is demanded [response]. It is a pattern we ourselves *must* attempt to follow.

• From the day of Pentecost the fledgling church is identified by its *response* to the Spirit, who gave the enhanced gift of speech to what Dominic Crossan appositely calls "a group of nobodies." Because of that, everyone—foreigners, outsiders, other "nobodies"—was enabled to hear. These people received a call mediated *through their own language.* Darkly, we are told that not everyone was equally impressed, and "some people laughed it off" (2:13). There are always some like that.

• Peter addressed the people with an extraordinary promise: "[Y]ou will receive the gift of the Holy Spirit" (2:38). Later, before the Sanhedrin, he was again clearly "filled with the Holy Spirit" (4:8). Then the whole community was "filled with the Holy Spirit and spoke the word of God with boldness" (4:31). The sequence is clear: call (illustrated by the gift of the Spirit), followed by pastoral response.

• As the number of disciples increased and food distribution needed be assured, the Twelve called a meeting to choose appropriate ministers "full of the Spirit and of wisdom" (6:3), that is, called by God and thereby enabled to produce the fitting response. Stephen distinguished himself, and the people "could not withstand…the Spirit with which he spoke" (6:10). After Stephen's death, Peter and John went to Samaria, and as their very first pastoral act they "prayed for [the Samaritans] that they might receive the Holy Spirit" (8:15), and they did.

- In the house of Cornelius (10:34ff), Peter experienced another chapter of his unfolding conversion, coming to realize that God calls the most unexpected people in the most unexpected places: that *who* and *where* one is are important. His insight became the inspiration for others, for "while Peter was still speaking, the Holy Spirit fell upon all who heard the word. The circumcised believers who had come with Peter were astounded that the gift of the Holy Spirit had been poured out even on the Gentiles" (10:44–45). Then their astonishment gave way to awe and respect when they saw the response of these pagans: they were evangelizing, proclaiming the greatness of God (10:46). Peter, meanwhile, continued trying to suppress his own astonishment that God was calling virtually anyone, anywhere! (11:12–17).
- God's call came to the pagans through the instrumentality of Barnabas and Paul, and the pagans were so convinced of God's action that they clearly identified the words of the apostles as the call of God: "When the Gentiles heard this, they were glad and praised the word of the Lord; and as many as had been destined for eternal life became believers. Thus the word of the Lord spread throughout the region" (13:48–49).

Not that God's plan is always unequivocal, or that believers do not have to weigh their own plans and intuitions in order to discern whether they represent God's will. In Acts we also learn what happens when disciples subordinate their own understanding to God's providential intentions, or when a pastoral plan builds on an initiative rather than a growing response to the Spirit. "They went through the region of Phrygia and Galatia, *having been forbidden by the Holy Spirit to speak the word in Asia.* When they had come opposite Mysia, they attempted to go into Bithynia, but *the Spirit of Jesus did not allow them;* so, passing by Mysia, they went down to Troas" (16:6–8).

How on earth can we come to that kind of obedience to the Spirit? How can we subordinate our best intuitions to God's inspiration, and even have the capacity to commit ourselves and yet be flexible enough to respond to totally unexpected movements of God's grace?

Your Will, Not Mine

Each of us is challenged to examine our life carefully in light of our professed belief in an apparent paradox: on the one hand we want to claim that God calls us specifically as individuals and that the call invites us to new enterprises during the course of a life that is always changing; on the other hand we know we might be wrongly identifying our own lifestyle as a true response to God's grace. The danger of confusion or delusion is considerable.

Gethsemane was only one place where Jesus needed to test his own intuitions in order to discern the conformity of his will with that of his "Abba." The desert was another, where he was tempted by Satan's siren voice. Luke describes the circumstances: "Jesus, *full of the Holy Spirit,* returned from the Jordan and was *led by the Spirit* in the wilderness" (Lk 4:1). Having discerned the true call and demonstrated an authentic, godly response, "Jesus, *filled with the power of the Spirit,* returned to Galilee" (4:14), continuing his ministry which was from first to last the expression of a covenantal relationship with God. Approaching the climax of his life on earth, Jesus in Gethsemane appears to have been both challenged and affirmed as his response and God's call converged. We must strive for the same convergence. Our tradition assures us that we will never be without the guiding Spirit, and that we will continue the work of Jesus and accomplish "greater works than these" (Jn 14:12).

"Peace is my gift to you," promised Jesus; but "not as the world gives it." In that discourse after the Last Supper, Jesus was addressing *"anyone"* and not only those actually present. He promised that anyone who loves him will keep his word, that is, respond to his impulse; and he made explicit the relationship implied: "My father will love [anyone], and we will come to [anyone] and make our home with [anyone]" (Jn 14: 23). It is in this context that Jesus promised peace (14:26–27).

Sometimes we can persuade ourselves that we are responding to the urging of another when we are actually driven by our own agenda. Furthermore, many of us imagine that if we were somewhere else or someone else we could more readily encounter God. Such thinking will sooner or later breed a lack of peace within us. The fruit of a genuine response to God's call is the peace that Jesus promised, and the presence of that peace in our lives will be the primary criterion by which we judge whether our will conforms with God's. Peace is neither "the quiet life" nor an absence of pain or difficulty or confusion. As it is promised by Jesus, *peace is a gift of the Spirit.* It resides in the deepest part of the soul where no turmoil reaches. Storms may rage above, but authentic peace can underpin lives which are a true response to the God who calls.

With peace comes God's liberating hand which frees from fear. "Do not be afraid" is said to occur 365 times in the Bible—one for every day of the year. If that is encouraging for the fearful, it is also a reminder that fear does tend to stalk us through life. The consolation is that as we respond increasingly to God's call, we are weaned from our fears and nourished on God's words of life. Jesus is the answer to our fears, even though they will not be entirely overcome before the Parousia.

Called, like Peter, to "put out into the deep water" (Lk 5:4), rather than being confined to life's shallows; called indeed to do the impossible, to come to Jesus across the waters (Mt 14:28), our lives will be permanently changed by our encounter with the one who calls in order to send, who heals by "restoration" (Mk 3:5) in order to commission. It is a risky venture, but risk was an essential ingredient of the vitality of the early Christian centuries, when to be a disciple was anything but respectable or undemanding, and the shortest route to insecurity if not premature death. Yet part of the legacy of the Spirit, and one of the four cardinal ("hinge") virtues, is prudence, a fitting companion for a faith-filled risktaker.

Prudence that repudiates all risk is counterfeit. It will keep us in the boat and not responsive to the impossible call of Jesus to leave the boat and walk on the water. Risk though, without a measure of prudence, becomes sheer foolhardiness. It will mark us as shallow and immature. Jesus warned Peter of the test ahead ("Satan has his wish to sift you all like wheat"), and of his own earnest prayers on Peter's behalf. And Peter's brash and unconsidered "Lord, I am ready to go with you to prison and to death!" is met by "I tell you, Peter, the cock will not crow this day, until you have denied three times that you know me" (Lk 22:33–34). Prudence is the wise companion of risk.

A further measure of the integrity of our response is that we are committed to a continuous process of discernment and constant renewal. An authentic response may change over time: the response of a healthy twenty-five-year-old is surely different in important respects from that of the same person as an infirm fifty-year-old or a sprightly octogenarian. Why? Because the subject has changed. And because God calls us as we are and where we are, and the call is respectful of the person.

Choose Life

Trying honestly and generously, with a blend of prudence and idealism (risk), to respond to the God who calls, we may ask: where is my vitality, my source of strength and energy? God calls us to life: our response should be to choose life (Deut 30:19). This is not self-indulgence—nor is it to deny the God of Life or the life of God within us. We need to know what saps and depletes us, what demeans or dehumanizes us, and how to respond to God's call to life.

Accordingly, we must discern our own limitations and boundaries. Not in order to remain confined or to refuse the challenge to transcend our limitations, but so that we do not play God or become caught in the hubris which would persuade us that we can do anything. We cannot. There is a savior and redeemer, and we are not the one! The generous-hearted and those who try to please everyone and do everything may be prone to a certain grandiosity of spirit. But this is not the Holy Spirit of God, who is a Spirit of gentleness and mildness and wisdom and fortitude and knowledge and justice.

So who are our companions in the process of discernment? Whom can we trust and who will both challenge and support our searching and our efforts to respond appropriately? We noted already the importance of a spiritual director or soul-friend— they can be the air beneath the wings of all who would take flight, the extra breath or last ounce of strength for all who strive to choose life. To know our limitations is the beginning of wisdom, but we may occasionally need a realistic challenge from someone who knows us intimately. Then we may produce a graced and creative response which will engage us with God's Spirit who renews the face of the earth.

We also need to understand the significance of our own embodiment. When our bodies permanently fail, we will be in a state so utterly different from our current circumstances that we simply cannot imagine it. Therefore, while we are in our bodies, we would do well to acknowledge, to cherish, and to utilize our embodied selves in a way consistent with our response to God's call. An unholy masochism and an imprudent disregard for or even repudiation of our embodiment appears to characterize many well-intentioned Christians. We need to examine the theology or spirituality which underpins such attitudes and behaviors. We have to ask how appropriate such attitudes and behaviors may be for people who believe not only that God chose Mary to embody Jesus, but that Jesus was embodied as fully human, and, specifically, fully male. We return to this topic later.

What Next?

Our Christian response is never an intellectual exercise or a coldly rational act. After all our preparations, we still do not know the outcome of the call or the cost of our response. We walk by faith. As disciples, we will always walk by faith. But our journey will never do violence to who we are, to where we are, or to the integrity of our lives. There may be violence—scandalously there is, and Christians are not immune—but God will not violate us, for God is a loving God. Disintegration may mark our lives, but God will not destroy our integrity, for our God has called us from the womb and dedicated us (Jer 1:5). Even if, absurdly, a mother should abandon her child, God will never abandon us (Isa 49:15). This, too, is our faith. We may need to cling to it.

Though violence surrounds us, if God's peace is within us, we put our hand to the plow and do not look back (Lk 9:62), we run the race and finish the course (2 Tim 4:7), we continue to love (1 Cor 13) and to remain faithful (Acts 2:42–45). And the God who will not ask more that we can handle, will do amazing things to and for those who trust:

[God] gives power to the faint, and strengthens the powerless. Even youths will faint and be weary, and the young will fall exhausted; but those who wait for the LORD *shall renew their strength, they shall mount up with wings like eagles, they shall run and not be weary, they shall walk and not faint* (Isa 40:29–31).

This we believe. May God help our unbelief. But before we proceed, let us remember the polar bear in London…. How will we continue to learn and to grow, to read the clouds, to know who we are and who we are called to be?

Chapter Two

Ministry As Mission

Where does the messenger stand? He cannot simply repeat the message he has heard. He has to understand the message, to interpret it, translate, contextualize, and elaborate it, and justify all these procedures.

VINCENT CRAPANZANO

Without charity, an evangelizing zeal will take on the guise of a will to power, a desire to universalize one's self-image.

EBOUSSI BOULAGA

Not a single missionary [in Latin America] was aware that the God the church proclaimed was a cultural image. The essence of idolatry is the identification of the reality of God with the image of God produced by a culture.

LEONARDO BOFF

Liberating Language

"Missionary zeal" is a phrase that may be so contaminated as to be unusable. It may connote well-meaning but objectionable interference with the lives of faraway people; and it may conjure up members of an exclusive, exotic, and possibly extreme group of religious zealots. While avoiding the phrase, we will try to retrieve an understanding of mission. Properly understood, *missionary* is a very apt description for every Christian who responds to God's call. *Mission* has been falsely polarized against *ministry*. And the only way to use the word *missionary* appropriately is by understanding that before we can apply it to ourselves, we must understand that first it describes Jesus.

To clarify some of these issues we must ponder the relationship between baptism and mission. Then we can identify the false distinction between missionaries and (ordinary) Christians, and between mission and (ordinary) ministry.

Called by God

Some believers are quite certain they are called by God, a conviction agnostics find either impressive or highly irritating! For those who struggle with life's meaning and purpose, it can be very inspiring to meet a person of strong convictions, whose doubts seem trivial; but to encounter people whose personal creed leads them to ride roughshod over the rights and sensibilities of others can be not only irritating but frankly offensive. Surely a call from God should not make a person offensive.

Despite negative connotations clustering round the word *missionary*, Vatican II reiterated that to be Christian is to be missionary, and that mission is intrinsic to Christianity (*Ad Gentes*, 2). Some claim bluntly that unless ministry is missionary in nature it is inauthentic. This raises a number of considerations for anyone claiming a personal call from God, and indeed anyone attempting to discern how to become a better Christian.

Some broad questions underlie this chapter. For example, how are people's rights and responsibilities related? How might the Good News be received as liberating and enlightening, rather than incomprehensible, meaningless, or even rankly offensive? Can Christians be people of true dialogue? And most fundamentally: if God does indeed call and send people and we honestly try to respond to the call, what are some of the implications?

To read the clouds intelligibly we must first look at what Jesus attempted and what he called and commissioned his followers to undertake. If our conclusions are more disturbing and challenging, more radical than we previously imagined, that may be because we are taking ourselves and God very seriously.

Some people seem to think that discerning the Christian call is a simple matter. But not everyone considers the context and the sensibilities, not to mention the basic human rights of those whose lives are affected as a result. History is full of disgraceful examples of self-righteous Christians who acted as though their own convictions about God's call justified their ill-treatment of others. God, we can be sure, does not call anyone to act unjustly (Mic 6:8).

The message Jesus proclaimed was never a blunt instrument: more a balm to soothe, or a key to people's hearts. Jesus never belittled the person, whether grieving widow, hemorrhaging woman, blind Bartimaeus, or diminutive Zacchaeus. Time and again, as we carefully watch his encounters with unlikely people, we note that he first calls and then commissions them. To be commissioned is to be sent: *co-missioned.* But the first movement of Jesus is to gather and call people: "Follow me, and I will make you fish for people" (Mt 4:19). Even when they are sent, it is not randomly. Nor is it to do whatever they deem useful. Luke is clear about the mission: the Twelve are sent to proclaim and to heal (Lk 9:2); the seventy-two are sent in pairs, "to every town and place where he [Jesus] himself intended to go" (Lk 10:1). In general terms, the disciples' mission is to replicate the work of Jesus. As for Jesus, in John's Gospel he insists that it was not his whim, but that he himself was sent (Jn 6:29, 44; 7:28; 12:44–45). Jesus

maintained that he did nothing of his own initiative but everything in dialogue with God (Jn 7:16; 14:24). This is critically
important for ourselves.

What exactly did Jesus undertake then, and what is the relation between what we do and what he did? "I have come that
they may have life, and have it abundantly" (Jn 10:10), said the
Good Shepherd. But the phrase "I have come" is put on the lips
of Jesus several times, and it points to *a variety of purposes*: he
had not come to abolish but to fulfill (Mt 5:17), not to call the
virtuous but sinners (Mt 9:13; Mk 2:17; Lk 5:32), not to bring
only peace (Jn 14:27) but a sword (Mt 10:34), and to set an individual and a family at odds (Mt 10:35; Lk 12:51–53). "I have come
in my Father's name" (Jn 5:43); and "not to do my own will, but
the will of him who sent me" (Jn 6:38). He came to comfort the
afflicted (and as Reinhold Niebuhr and Dorothy Day added, to
afflict the comfortable). His mission was to help people to live
fully, to offer a quite new level of life, to transform expectations,
and to offer hope and the possibility of transcendence to those
whose lives are bowed down.

Perhaps the best summary of his mission is the prophetic description which Jesus reads from the scroll in the synagogue, at
the very outset of his ministry. Luke's Gospel records the words
of Isaiah:

> *The Spirit of the Lord is upon me,*
> *because he has anointed me to bring good news to the poor.*
> *He has sent me to proclaim release to the captives*
> *and recovery of sight to the blind, to let the oppressed go free,*
> *to proclaim the year of the Lord's favor* (Lk 4:18–19).

If we gloss this passage, we might render it like this: *The breath
or Spirit of God has…consecrated me with oil of gladness…to announce good news to the poorest of the depressed poor; has sent me*

to make whole, to wrap or swaddle those whose hearts are crushed; to publish news of pardon and remission for prisoners of war, nobodies and exiles; to be a herald of restoration of vision to those whose eyes are dim; to rehabilitate the bruised; to proclaim a Happy New Year of God's Jubilee. This *is* ornate, yet faithful to the sense of the Greek and Hebrew texts. It conveys some idea of how exciting and hopeful and good is the Good News we so often talk about. But the passage has become perhaps too well known, and may have lost some of its effectiveness. But good news is not *predictable,* and we need to rekindle the excitement contained in these lines if we are to be fired by it and to excite others.

Ministry and Mission in Matthew and Luke

Jesus' proclamation in the synagogue at Nazareth is like a personal job description and mission statement rolled into one. Yet when asked to describe the essential task of the Christian today, some Christians, including those who describe themselves as missionaries, may not even think of this passage, much less apply it to themselves. A more familiar reference is in Matthew's Gospel, a classic text to which generations of Christians have returned. It seems simple and clear, though it is complex and nuanced, as David Bosch (1991) pointed out.

The eleven disciples set out for Galilee, to the mountain where Jesus had arranged to meet them. When they saw him they fell down before him, though some hesitated. Jesus came up and spoke to them. He said: "All authority in heaven and on earth has been given to me. Go, therefore, make disciples of all the nations; baptize them in the name of the Father and of the Son and of the Holy Spirit, and teach them to observe all the commands I gave you. And know that I am with you always; yes, to the end of time" (Mt 28:16–20).

There are several points to ponder. First, the passage was written years after the event. Second, words spoken by Jesus himself are actually directed at the eleven disciples. Most importantly, the context is post-Resurrection: what Jesus himself did earlier—his own daily ministry—is not described here. Finally, the text neither describes what was expected of the sinners and the sick who were forgiven, healed, and commissioned, nor what is expected of ourselves today.

Must we conclude that after the Resurrection the mission that Jesus himself had exemplified by his public ministry was radically changed, or even that the ministry of Jesus himself was not missionary? Did mission only begin after the Resurrection?

The mandate identified in Matthew 28 is centrifugal, magisterial, and exclusive. It is centrifugal for it commands the disciples to move from where they are, to go forth, to leave the center which they currently occupy, and go to the edge. It is magisterial [*magister*, a person of substance: master or teacher] inasmuch as it explicitly urges the disciples to *teach*. It is exclusive, strictly speaking, because it addresses only the eleven surviving apostles.

This passage has been invoked over the centuries to buttress and justify the Christian missionary enterprise, particularly in its magisterial, clerical, and exclusive form. Historically, the emphasis of the missionary movement has been overwhelmingly one way, from "here" to "there" and from "us" to "them." The eleven (and descendants by apostolic succession) are understood to be the donors, while "the nations" are the recipients. The mission is to "teach," "baptize," and "make disciples." The justification has appeared incontestably clear: Jesus says "Go!" and "I am with you."

It would be inappropriate to soften hard sayings or to render a biblical passage politically correct. But if we place alongside this passage both the self-professed mission of Jesus in Luke 4:18–19, and the invitation he expressly extends to his followers, then we must acknowledge other important dynamics. The oft-repeated word of call, "come," in contrast to the centrifugal "go," is *centripetal* (seeking the center, moving away from the edge); the injunction to "follow me" (for "I am meek and humble of heart") is not magisterial but ministerial [*minister*: a person of little substance, small, subordinate, an attendant]; and the very stance of Jesus is truly servantlike or "humble" [*hum-*: of the earth, fertile, productive], for he does not lord it over anyone but occupies the same ground on which they stand. Then he can look straight into their eyes.

There is still work to be done if today's followers of Jesus are to allow the message of both Matthew 28 and Luke 4 to be a source of disturbance and challenge.

From Ministry to Mission

For a generation or more there have been intermittent skirmishes and sometimes quite serious conflicts between those who want to separate the notions of mission and ministry, and those who see them as complementary, intrinsically related, and theoretically inseparable.

Perhaps because of certain apparent implications of mission, some Christians have maintained (or been persuaded) that the term certainly does not apply to them, particularly if their activity does not involve "the nations." Even the Vatican II assertion of the intrinsically missionary nature of the Church has not appreciably affected the lives of many. Indeed, if *mission* and *missionary* are defined geographically or by ordination and specialization, it will be difficult to persuade most baptized Christians that mission is an imperative directed at all Christians. But if the life and invitation of Jesus are the yardstick, then it may be possible and worthwhile to revisit the ministry/mission debate, with a view to reading the clouds in our times.

Jesus never operated in an exclusive fashion, and his life's work was not so much a clearly defined or neat program, as a rather open-ended or messy undertaking. We know how widely he cast his net, and that no one was excluded except those who excluded themselves. Indeed, his whole approach directly favored those who were excluded or who felt themselves to be (Nolan, 1992). In recent times we have come to identify this as Jesus' *preferential option for the poor*. Such a pastoral plan cannot possibly be fixed or static: it must be open-ended and dynamic. It must be bounteously centrifugal.

The activity of Jesus and of his disciples is characterized by a boundary-breaking outreach, a centrifugal dynamic. The disciples first experience a call to the center, just as Jesus experienced the conviction that he was sent by the Father whose call he had heard (Mk 1:11). At the outset of his public life, we encounter Jesus, briefly the center of attraction, working many miracles and healing many people. On the next day Peter approaches Jesus, apparently with a very attractive entrepreneurial plan: he will act as an agent for Jesus! But Jesus is having none of it: "Let us go on to the neighboring country towns, so that I can proclaim the message there also; for *that is what I came out to do*" (Mk 1:38). Just as Jesus is moving from the center, so Peter and others must be challenged and propelled into the surrounding countryside, for that is the momentum of mission.

Some have tried to argue that Jesus was not a true missionary since he confined himself to his own people, and that true mission only happened after the Ascension. This ignores the insights that the very mission of Jesus seems to have become clearer to him through his encounters with other people (Crossan, 1991): some of them, like the Canaanite woman (Mt 15:2ff) or the centurion (Mt 8:5ff), even seem to have called him beyond and through his own comfort zone ("the lost sheep of the House of Israel"), but most were encountered on the margins and the edges of normal or respectable life. His ministry became both centrifugal and "eccentric": not bogged down, always on the move, taking place outside the centers of power, influence, and respectability.

Much later, on the day of Pentecost, the centrifugal force of the Holy Spirit propelled the disciples from the center (the Upper Room) to the edge, "to the ends of the earth" (Acts 1:8). That momentum is sustained as the history of fledgling Christianity unfolds. Paul and Barnabas exemplify it well. They justify themselves by claiming that they must be peripatetic, *en route*, initially among the Jewish people and then beyond: "For so the Lord has commanded us, saying, 'I have set you to be a light for the Gentiles, so that you may bring salvation to the ends of the earth'" (Acts 13:47).

The ministry of Jesus and of his followers is always outgoing, embracing, inclusive. In Jesus, ministry and mission are one. And as it was with the disciples after the Resurrection, so, by extension, it should be with ourselves. Jesus promised, "You will receive power when the Holy Spirit has come upon you; and you will be my witnesses in Jerusalem, in all Judea and Samaria, and to the ends of the earth" (Acts 1:8). Confirmation by the Spirit at Pentecost, and ours through the sacraments of initiation, provides momentum and justification for a ministry of inclusive outreach. Ministry makes no essential distinctions based on geography. In the early church there was not even a special word to designate missionary: there was absolutely no need for it; the ministry of Christians was as outgoing, embracing, and inclusive as that of Jesus. Ministry was mission!

Some people maintain that if everything is mission, nothing is mission. The logic of this assertion, I must admit, escapes me! Certainly, in the course of Christian history, a false distinction or opposition has been made between ministry and mission; a wedge has been driven between what is not separated or polarized in the life and work of Jesus and his early followers. This wedge is a creation of the historical, institutionalized, hierarchical church which came to be patterned on the Roman Imperial State and not on the model of Jesus. If there were a restoration of all things in Christ in our own day, all authentic ministry would have a missionary character, and far from saying that nothing is mission, we might be astounded at the full potential of contemporary Christian ministry in the spirit of Christ!

Before that, however, we need to deconstruct our cherished or preconceived ecclesiastical thinking and then reconstruct a centrifugal and eccentric or marginal ministry in the Spirit of Jesus.

Here, There, Everywhere

Mission implies movement, but not only to exotic places. Saint Thérèse of Lisieux is a patroness of what used to be called "the missions," though her adult life was short and monastic. If mission were determined by length of time, or distance from one's birthplace, we would have to draw some strange conclusions. The kind of movement demanded of a true missionary ministry is primarily a stretching, a breaking-of-boundaries for the sake of God's realm, and a movement of transcendence. This, of course, is quite well exemplified in the Little Flower of Lisieux, not to mention Jesus!

In order to branch out, a tree or plant must be rooted. To undertake a missionary ministry, a strong rootedness or sense of identity is required. The successful minister stretches without breaking and negotiates boundaries without losing integrity or compromising others'.

Self-actualization (the realizing of one's potential) is not to be overlooked. Yet the Christian mission is an invitation to move well beyond *self*-actualization, beyond the self, to nothing less than transcendence or transformation. The human potential is greatly constrained if a person concentrates on the self at the expense of the broader community (Friedan, 1993:621). Furthermore the Christian is called both to self-abnegation and self-transcendence, to the cross and the Resurrection. If we settle for reaching our potential we may aim too low, for we are called to become something entirely new: a new creation (2 Cor 5:17).

To have roots is not, of course, to be root-bound: that implies immobilization, fixity, being rooted to the spot. True missionary ministry is possible in principle for anyone open to the transforming inspiration of the Spirit which causes us to branch out. Geographically, Jesus did not go very far from home; but to suggest that his was not a missionary ministry is to misunderstand the Incarnation! In terms of outreach and inclusion, of branching out into encounters with others, Jesus went to the ends of the earth. This is the nature of his ministry, the reason for the Incarnation.

We are called as we are and where we are; then we are sent, in a movement of transformation ("trans-formation": being formed anew in the process of crossing over) to become new persons through new encounters. We may contribute to the transformation of others, but that is only part of mission. Also essential but sometimes overlooked is the fact that through the Spirit of God we ourselves are being transformed. The process of engaging in the centrifugal, eccentric excitement of evangelization may not take us very far from home; but in terms of taking us far from where we are and making us far from who we are (ontologically), it will take us to the ends of the earth.

A Priestly People to Serve Our God

Christians are called to struggle with sinful propensities and to try to penetrate the formidable boundaries of personal narrowness, comfort, and prejudice. Yet this agenda is only a means to an end. It is intended to turn the believer inside out, to engage us with the wider community, to make us our brothers' and sisters' keepers. Still, for many people, a major problem remains: they feel they cannot be missionary in what they consider the primary sense, either because they are not full-time or because they are not theologically trained or anointed with the sacrament of priestly ordination. Such an attitude needs to be challenged and changed, and urgently!

Lay mission and *lay missionary* are widely used terms, and for understandable reasons. Initially, they were used in order to invite the response of all the baptized. But if they actually polarize the Christian community, they have become less than helpful. That polarization has been happening over the past thirty years or so. Vatican II identified the whole church as the people of God *(Ad Gentes,* 10–18), a priestly people by virtue of common baptism. Baptism incorporates us, makes us members of the Body of Christ and of the corporation of Christians. That corporation is a missionary community, called and sent, individually and collectively, from varied particular contexts, to continue the work of Jesus for the benefit of the whole of humankind without exception. Notwithstanding the highly problematic and controversial language of *Ad Gentes,* 10–18, lay mission cannot logically be *essentially* different from any other variety: all missionary ministry is a participation in that of Jesus (Weakland, 1997:13–15).

Recent biblical scholarship has produced many new insights about the life and ministry of Jesus (Crossan 1991; Malina 1981, 1986, 1992; Meier 1994, Neyrey 1991). Theological thinking has reflected on these insights, which have emphasized the essentially *kenotic* (or selfless) emptying ministry of Jesus and his servant-leadership. The result has been further clarity about the revolutionary nature of Jesus' agenda. The first and last, the greatest and least, shall exchange places; those who have will lose, and those who have nothing will gain; status will count for nothing, and adults must become children; outcasts will be gathered in and the privileged will be scattered; leadership is by serving. All of this, in turn, provides a radical challenge to every Christian, and an incentive to join more fully in the "Jesus-society."

The people of God are not undifferentiated, of course: in the Body of Christ there are different gifts and different tasks, and Saint Paul is both clear and lyrical about this. But always it is "the same Spirit" and "the same Lord" working in various ways and myriad people; "the same God…activates all of them [the different gifts] in everyone" (1 Cor 12:5–6). This Spirit, given to us at baptism, is the same Spirit who brought order from chaos, who hovered over Jesus at the Jordan and led him into and out of the desert, into whose hands Jesus commended his last breath, and whom Jesus promised as the Comforter and Inspirer of continued generations of believers!

The unity of mission does not require that we standardize all Christians or deny all differences; but it is not found by creating authoritarian hierarchy or canonizing differences. The unity is in the Spirit, constantly attracting everyone to God's embrace and loving us equally, not because of who we are but because God does not have favorites (Deut 10:17).

Elephants in captivity can be restrained very cheaply. If a baby elephant is tethered it will soon discover its limitations and not resist the tether. Though it grows to be amazingly strong, as long as it remains tethered each day or night, it will never realize its true power. The tether would be no match for an undomesticated elephant, but a beast in captivity simply does not know its own strength. How different is the action of the Spirit of Jesus, who sets free and inspires all of the people of God—provided they are realistically humble and Spirit-led. The kingdom proclaimed by Jesus is modeled on radical equality, and the Spirit who renews the face of the earth is calling us to be transformed rather than tethered. We have no business trying to tether the Spirit, and God's Spirit will surely not tether the faithful, but will lead them to enjoy great and God-given strength.

Church and Kingdom

If the motive for mission is the creation and maintenance of the church, mission will be essentially concerned with baptism and church-extension. But if the focus is the kingdom or realm of God, then without compromising the significance of the gift of baptism nor the importance of visible communities of baptized people, there is less likelihood of restricting mission to church-extension. This referent may be obvious now, but historically the two have been far too closely identified.

Jesus was utterly committed to God's realm (kingdom), and called people to a similar commitment, urging us all to pray to God, may "your kingdom come...on earth as it is in heaven" (Mt 6:10). We can pray for this in word, but also through our whole attitude and lifestyle. If increasing church membership through baptism is the major pastoral issue, then most of the current membership of the church cannot be directly involved, and mission indeed becomes an elitist and specialized pursuit. Of course, the church does call and authorize some to administer the formal sacraments, but mission cannot be limited to that task, since one simply cannot put limits around God's providential outreach. As Jesus said to would-be followers, "Let the dead bury their own dead; but as for you, go and proclaim the kingdom of God" (Lk 9:60). Each and all of us are called and sent to proclaim God's reign. This is mission, every bit as much as formally baptizing people.

A very strong image of the church used to be the "ark of salvation," the boat upon the waves, always searching for the drowning souls, always prepared to let down the nets and rescue the half dead. Taken to its limits such a metaphor calls for an exceedingly large boat, a limited number of people, or a very unfair arrangement!

In recent years, particularly, some theologians began to voice the opinion that, rather than the church being the *normal* means of salvation, it might be more appropriately called the *abnormal* means. After all, in the centuries before Jesus the church simply did not exist. And, in the contemporary world, hardly one-third of humanity is nominally Christian (Barrett, 1998). An absolute majority of the world's population, therefore, could never expect to encounter the church or learn Christian teachings.

As the prevailing metaphor (the church as *lifeboat*) proved less persuasive, the stage was set for new ones. Among others, the church as *sacrament of salvation* (*AG*, 1; *LG*, 48; *Catechism*, 1994: 776) has proved helpful. However, we should neither repudiate metaphors with a distinguished history, nor take any metaphor literally. But the relationship between church and kingdom is still a matter of serious discussion and heated debate *(LG*, 14).

In 1990, Pope John Paul II addressed the issue concretely in *Redemptoris Missio*, the encyclical on the Church's missionary activity *(RM* 20–22, 26). He declared that to imagine one could proclaim the kingdom of God without at the same time proclaiming the church is not legitimate. While they are not identical, neither should church and kingdom be opposed. *Dialogue and Proclamation*, issued almost simultaneously, pursued some of these critical issues *(DP*, 33–36, 58–59).

Yet questions remain: Who, then, may proclaim the kingdom, and how? Is proclamation of the kingdom identical with proclamation of the church? And what about the *normal/abnormal* means of salvation? Though there is no single, simple, generally accepted answer to any of these questions, their very formulation indicates a developing agenda for those who want to respond to Christ and to their baptism, as well as to the church and perhaps to their priestly ordination and religious institutional charism. But it is surely unacceptable and unbiblical to exclude or marginalize from the mission of the church those who are not ordained; and it is just as clear that "outside the church, no salvation" simply cannot mean what once it was accepted to mean.

The church, sacrament of salvation, stands as a beacon or a signpost to the kingdom of God. The church is not the kingdom. But all baptized people, by the witness of their lives can proclaim a kingdom of inclusion and forgiveness and justice and equality, and they can do so as Jesus did, and in the name of Jesus, until he comes again. This is not to demean mission, so much as to make it possible for all. If some presume that their lives speak louder and that their witness is more worthy, perhaps the parable of the Laborers in the Vineyard (Mt 20:1–16) may be an appropriate corrective.

Proclamation, Dialogue, Witness, Liberation

Empirically, not everyone in the church is called to baptize. Realistically, not everyone in the world has been called to be baptized. Vocationally, however, every Christian *is* called to mission. All baptized persons, truly attentive to their conscience (the voice of God), and trying to act justly, love tenderly, and walk humbly with God (Mic 6:8) are helping to usher in God's kingdom. Practically speaking, for most people in the world the realm of God may be more accessible than is the church. So for those who belong to the People of God, what are some of the implications of their membership?

The fact that we have different gifts does not mean that Christians are responding to fundamentally different callings. The sheer fact that there are many different people does not imply that we are marked by *essential* differences. In Christ, the obvious differences between persons do not merit moral distinctions (Rom

3:22; 10:12; Gal 3:26), for we are all one in Christ. So how, in Christ, can we engage in missionary ministry, whoever and wherever we are?

Evangelization is the reason Jesus came; it is what he undertook. In recent years, the word has been broken open to disclose a number of different components. Literally, it means "goodnews-ing" or "good-news-ation." It is helpful to approach this complex reality in terms of its four constituents: proclamation, dialogue, witness, and liberation (*SEDOS Seminar*, Rome 1981: in Jenkinson and O'Sullivan, eds., 1989). All of these are essential; none has absolute priority. We will examine them in turn. But evangelization—the mission of Jesus and the mission of his followers—is a communal, *ecclesial* undertaking. It cannot be executed totally by any individual. Nor is the church reducible to a single person such as pope or bishop: it is the *People of God,* all members of whom have responsibility and voice (*AG,* Chapter 2). The challenge is for people of faith to work together, and together to undertake *all* of the imperatives of mission. So it would be a travesty of evangelization for a priest to baptize hordes of people and leave them without the word of God, the Eucharist, the witness of Christian life, or the moral support of the wider Christian community. But likewise, to engage in intellectually stimulating dialogue about religion, yet with neither desire nor attempt to proclaim the God of Jesus Christ and the Incarnate One, would not be true mission.

Proclamation: "Jesus came to Galilee, proclaiming the good news of God, and saying, 'The time is fulfilled, and the kingdom of God has come near; repent, and believe in the good news'" (Mk 1:14–15). Proclamation is familiar to us in its most explicit form: the systematic announcement of the gospel. Nevertheless, proclamation is not the whole of evangelization; it is not the prerogative of clergy alone; and it is an imperative for the whole People of God.

Proclamation, of course, is prominent in the Matthew 28 passage which we identified with a classical understanding of evangelization. Through the centuries, the prerogative of *formal proclamation* has been clerically claimed and clung to, while the laity were left with little but the crumbs of evangelization. Such an intolerable situation is not entirely a thing of the past, but the injustice has been identified and is being addressed. *Every* community of Christians has the responsibility and thus the right to proclaim the Good News, in various ways and according to circumstances. The proclamation cannot and must not simply be left to others. Baptism calls each of us.

Dialogue: A rather curious business, dialogue evokes a range of reactions. To some people, it connotes a thinly veiled attempt to proselytize. Others understand it primarily as an intellectual exchange. Those who hold to the classical formula "error has no rights" are very suspicious of dialogue: it has no place in evangelization. Finally, dialogue is treated by some as a kind of interreligious diplomacy. So what is its theological nature? What is it for? What does it accomplish?

If we are trying to read the clouds rather than simply to argue or justify a position, we will know that unless our whole life is cast as dialogue, then any particular dialogues we undertake, formally or informally, will not meet the criteria of Jesus. Authentic dialogue requires the engagement of several people in a common undertaking: it is relational before it is programmatic or agenda-based. Jesus was more likely to start a dialogue with "what do you want me to do?" or "give me a drink" than with "listen to me." Only if we are committed to a *dialogue of life,* a fusing of the message we proclaim with the one we embody and live, are we following Jesus.

This is not to diminish the importance of dialogue. And it does not allow us either to mask it under the guise of good works or subordinate it to any of the other components of evangelization. If dialogue is truly relational, it will be respectful of persons and circumstances. If it is an imperative of evangelization, it will not be reduced or subordinated to anything. Good news, like God, wants to become known. But dialogue, though sometimes explicit and sometimes implicit, sometimes formal and sometimes informal, will *always* lead to transformation: it will not leave either party quite the same. This is as clear in the encounters of Jesus with the woman at the well (Jn 4) or the Syrophoenician woman (Mk 7) as it is in the encounters of our own lives.

Years ago, when I first lived in Africa, a personal encounter left an indelible mark. The woman and myself were strangers. She was gentle, gracious, and silent. We shared no common language, nor a common faith. She would come to my house and sit, still and silent, for an hour or more in the evening, while I read or wrote. She was intimately present, utterly in relationship, and as surely in dialogue as if we had shared an animated conversation. The powerful simplicity of her moral support touched me deeply. She affected my life, causing me serious reflection on my own ministry. I must have affected hers, for she continued to come. We hardly shared a word beyond formal greetings. But we shared part of our lives.

The essential fruit or implication of dialogue is very well captured in the following passage. Here is a pastor of the Swiss Reformed Church:

Evangelization is martyria. That does not mean primarily the risking of possessions and life, but rather that we gamble, as it were, with our understanding of belief in the course of evangelizing. We, so to speak, submit our understanding of the world and of God and of our faith to the test of dialogue. We have no guarantee that our understanding of faith will emerge unaltered from that dialogue. On the contrary. How can we expect that those listening to us should be ready in principle to change their lives and ways of thinking if we, the evangelists, are not notionally prepared to submit to the same discipline? (Hollenweger, 1979: 40–41).

This text speaks of *submitting one's understanding* of the world (and of God and our faith) to the test of dialogue. But we live in and pass through *many* worlds in the course of a lifetime. We grow and change, we encounter surprising people, and we revisit places as if for the first time. This is part of the challenge we face as we try to interpret life, read the clouds, and apply each day's lessons to our changing and unfolding lives. There is transformation in the air for all disciples of Christ. Dialogue should help transform us, and not simply the people we meet. After all, dialogue is not proselytization. And it is the Spirit, not ourselves, who enlightens and breathes—wherever the Spirit leads us!

Witness: The witness of one's whole life is as important as the dialogue of life. The key is integration. We must integrate our life with each component of evangelization. We must find a way to integrate the components themselves for they are like interlocking pieces. Consequently, what is said here about witness is said in the context of evangelization as a unified field.

Perhaps no component of evangelization is more prone to abuse or misrepresentation than witness. It may seem not to disturb a person's comfort or complacency, and it can appear to offer a theological justification for one's presence among others without challenging either party. So we must remember that witness is only one component of evangelization, and that we can certainly not reduce the mission statement of Jesus in Luke 4:18–19 to witness alone.

Circumstances sometime require that explicit proclamation be avoided, and perhaps some persons' gifts are not best employed in explicit proclamation or dialogue; but evangelical witness can never become a soft option or an excuse for ministerial laziness. Witness, like the other imperatives, needs to be embodied: if it is not through our words that we proclaim love and forgiveness and inclusion and the rest, then it must certainly be through the active witness of our lives.

In the late 1960s, I became friendly with a man I met in Edinburgh, Scotland. He was a homeless street person and ex-convict; I was a young priest and university student. We got on famously. Trained in the use of explosives, he had spent five years in the British Army, happily blowing things up. In 1945 he was given a new suit, a little money, and sent to seek fame and fortune! His only skill involved explosives. And so it was that he took to a life outside the law—a life of blowing up safes. Badly. By 1970, with dozens of convictions, he had spent the equivalent of more than twenty of the previous twenty-five years behind bars. He had become so institutionalized, so unsuited to independent living, that he would "arrange" to get arrested soon after being released. From him I learned a little about listening and a lot about the capacity of the human stomach— his appetite was as prodigious as his tales were tall. And he was always hungry, no matter what time we met. We got on extremely well, and engaged in some mutual evangelical witness (Mt 25:35–36). But our informal yet real dialogue was critical to our friendship: he taught me that hierarchy and dialogue are incompatible. Both of our lives were changed by this graced encounter.

Liberation: This is a gospel imperative which may have been abused in our time, and has certainly been maligned and misrepresented. No one should have to apologize for being committed to liberation, and there is a serious need for any rhetoric about human dignity to be supported by such commitment. Liberation is after all, the most obvious of all the imperatives of evangelization, if we take Luke 4:18 as our criterion. It is about freedom, setting free, giving freely. It is about "liberty to captives" applying to all manner of captivity—enslavement, servitude, exploitation. It is about those strong biblical images—untying the thong, breaking the shackles, loosing the yoke. And it is subsequently offered freely by those who have received freely. As Jesus enjoined those he called and sent: "You received without payment, give without payment" (Mt 10:8). Yet how far have some of us fallen, by our grudging or miserly ministrations, or by the strings we have attached to our gifts?

To proclaim "liberty to captives" is empty rhetoric unless we offer moral support to people in addictive situations. To "set the downtrodden free" is a mere slogan unless we empower or ennoble people whose hearts or spirits are broken. To "give new sight to the blind" is a vain promise unless we offer vision, encourage insight, and remove blind spots. These are all examples of the liberation which Jesus proclaimed, in action as much as in word. They challenge us all, now, and urgently.

Inculturation

Each component of evangelization has equal claim; together they constitute "good-news-ing." But another aspect may not be omitted: inculturation. This refers to the way the gospel encounters a particular culture and calls that culture to be enriched, transformed. Increasingly, we recognize that every theology is a local theology, and that uniformity of theological expression is neither possible nor desirable. Inculturation thus becomes an imperative of evangelization. But rather than making it replace one of the four, or add it as a fifth, let us say that there is simply no authentic evangelization that is not also an inculturation. In other words, the universal church is a communion of local churches, and each local church is a community with its own identity and integrity, not cut off from other local churches but reaching out from its own center to encounter others on their thresholds or beyond the church's own borders. This is the only way to be church. It reminds us that images and expressions of church, no less than of cultures and societies and the world itself, are varied and changing, that none of us can claim a definitive understanding of church or people or cosmos, and that each of us must continue our apprenticeship in reading the clouds.

————

In the first chapter, we considered the call which God extends to every baptized person. This chapter has tried to characterize the field which stretches before us all: a field of ministry which is also a mission field. We have identified evangelization as the Jesus-approach or the Jesus-response to the call, and noted its components.

In *Part Two* we will look more closely at where our journey might lead as we commit ourselves to a closer following of Jesus. To the disciples concerned about whether he had eaten, he said: "My food is to do the will of the one who sent me, and to complete his work. Look around you, look at the fields; already they are white, white for harvest" (Jn 4:34–35). We, too, must look around, at the fields and above them, if we are to read the signs and the clouds, and follow the Master.

Part Two

———

INTEGRATING
LIFE
AND
MINISTRY

Chapter Three

Stories, Parables, and Pastoral Ministry

The goal is not to read a book; the goal is to read the story taking place all around us.

Brian Swimme and Thomas Berry

Some beautiful, sacred memory, preserved since childhood, is perhaps the best education of all. Even if only one good memory is left in our hearts, it may also be the instrument of our salvation one day.

Fyodor Dostoevsky

At the heart and core of the Christians' detachment from convention, lay a story.

Henry Chadwick

A Parable of Stories

Though life's path may be strewn with paradox and ambiguity, those who are led by the Spirit have a confidence to match any difficulty. They believe that as children of God (Rom 8:14) they

51

will never be abandoned, and that they have a covenantal relationship with God. But how in practice can we prepare for something that is both unknown and unfolding? How can we prepare for life-changing encounters with people we have never met?

Our identity, and that of others, is encoded in many ways: in language, but also in art and dance, ritual and play, in music and embodiment—the conventional or cultural way in which particular people present or display themselves. All these things need to be interpreted, for although meaning is found universally it must be sought and discovered locally. Meaning is always rooted and contextualized in *particular* languages and art forms, *particular* dances and rituals, and in *particular* persons.

The stories of people's lives provide access to their worlds of meaning, and the important stories of whole groups of people must be kept alive. Boring, meaningless, or self-indulgent stories will simply not survive very long. But those that have survived for generations will contain the rich seams of a people's identity, wisdom, and spirituality. Stories live, of course, in communities and not simply in texts.

None of us knows in detail where we will be called or to whom we will be sent in the course of a lifetime. But we can learn something about people, and about their wonderful variety, by learning their stories. How can we presume to read the clouds unless we can read the stories? Stories are the warp and woof of people's lives.

The undertaking does not even have to be tedious or academic; authentic stories have the power to excite and even inspire us. And as we perceive how wisdom is located in story, we may, in turn, reclaim some of our own stories, from our many different cultures and even from our biblical heritage. The result will be a deeper understanding of who we are, and a mutually enriching dialogue with others.

Memories and stories, music and song: the threads of human culture. Without them the fabric of life begins to fray and unravel until it falls like a pile of rags at our feet, leaving us exposed, bewildered, and traumatized. There was a time in Western history when that fabric was strong and durable. Families told stories and congregations sang songs, and people knew where they came from and where they were bound. Then the Age of Enlightenment succeeded in replacing myths and fairy tales with rational explanation and scientific truth. But if we gained some intellectual insight, we became, as a people, spiritually starved and emotionally emaciated. And now the damage is done. It is almost too late for psychology and theology and other disciplines to rehabilitate songs and stories, singers and narrators. Some people cannot remember, others have become deaf, and yet others appear to have lost their voice. In our times, Western Christianity and culture seems almost to have misplaced its soul. If Western theology is thriving, Christian ministry is in something of a mess. The collective unconscious of the West seems to have suffered a stroke. We have all but forgotten who we are or where we came from.

But all is not lost, for as long as memories and communities, poetry, drama, stories and song exist, there is still hope. Yet these are insufficient of themselves: there must be singers of songs and tellers of tales, listeners and chorus, learners and heroes.

This chapter tries to illustrate the importance of story by unlocking some of the wisdom to be found there. Our own social identity requires that we have some common narratives, some common stories. And our spirituality can be nourished by our sharing of stories. Storytelling by people of faith, whether by proclamation or dialogue, by ritualization or dance, in music or song or other forms of embodiment, can be an authentic form of ministry, for it can instruct, nourish, challenge, inspire, and build community. Others' stories may jog memories of our own half-forgotten stories. But others' stories may also be a revelation to us—of others' wisdom and spirituality.

A Hasidic Tale

When the great Rabbi, Israel Baal Shem Tov, saw misfortune threatening the Jews, it was his custom to go into a certain part of the forest to meditate. There he would light a candle, say a special prayer, and the miracle would be accomplished and misfortune averted.

Later, when his disciple, the celebrated Magid of Mezritch, had occasion for the same reason, to intercede with heaven, he would go to the same place in the forest and say: "Master of the Universe, listen! I do not know how to light the fire, but I am still able to say the prayers." And again the miracle would be accomplished.

Still later, Rabbi Moshe Leib of Sasov, in order to save his people once more, would go into the forest and say: "I do not know how to light the fire, I do not know the prayer, but I know the place and this must be sufficient." It was sufficient, and the miracle was accomplished.

Then it fell to Rabbi Israel of Rizhyn to overcome misfortune. Sitting in his armchair, his head in his hands, he spoke to God. "I am unable to light the fire and I do not know the prayer; I cannot even find the place in the forest. All I can do is to tell the story, and that must be sufficient." And it was sufficient. God made humankind because God loves stories (Wiesel, 1982).

There are two types of story: call them the epic and the local, the archetype and the reproduction, or the cosmic and the particular. But they are not to be completely separated, for they breathe life into and they draw life from each other.

The first type concerns the human pilgrimage. In Christian circles such stories tell of the *Pilgrim's Progress*, of *The Imitation of Christ*, or more generally of the people of the Way, or of the cross and Resurrection. But every culture will attempt to identify the "common project," the path to wisdom and peace. There is an urgent need for us to reclaim the memories and share the stories of the Epic of Redemption, for without them we will become isolated and hopeless. These are stories of the Creator's revelation in Jesus, of God's "Amazing Grace," of the Christian call and response, of our falling and rising yet our continued commitment to the dance of life. These stories can make and mold us, can remind us of covenant and of promise, can imbue us with hope and fortitude, and can bond us as a chosen people overflowing with Good News. Perhaps if we are more sensitive to the stories which touch our own identity, we might resonate with the stories of others.

For some people, the discovery process takes a different route, beginning in a far-off country and returning like the Prodigal Son to discover riches that were within reach all along. Since all Christians are called to be swept up in this common story, all of us together should converge and *concelebrate our common story*, affirm one another, and bless one another on the way. There is no room for unhealthy competitiveness, nor self-glorification, when it comes to telling stories of God's grace.

The second type consists of stories more local in scope, stories that remind us of closer loyalties: to family and friends, to societies and institutions, to communities and congregations. Everyone has a particular tale or story. Some stories may need to be declaimed for all to hear, others gently crooned to intimate friends. This one may demand frequent and loud publicity, while that one may require only occasional and quietly private recollection. But stories are not simply to be blurted out, nor allowed to become boring or self-serving. They have their own proper contexts, and they are also driven by the strength of narrative dynamics: by rules. And songs have their own appropriate times, and their special haunting and evocative melodies.

So who tells the stories and who sings the songs? And what stories and songs will be chosen and by whom? Families used to gather and tell stories, and communities created festivals and celebrations to ensure that stories did not die. As families or communities, we may have lost or forgotten many of our stories. But if we examine the composite wisdom of the human race over centuries and millennia, we can discover patterns and rules, meanings and wisdom, riches we have forgotten or never known. We may find in the mechanics of storytelling and the dynamics of song, the key we need in order to become liberated again. Then we can proceed, freer and more focused, to live and celebrate the dangerous and challenging memory of Jesus, because now we know a little better who we are and where we are bound, and who are our companions participating in the never-ending story that we call the Christian pilgrimage.

For millennia, traditional rites of passage have forged people into communities and strengthened them for the tasks and transitions and pains of life. Those who share experience and aspirations through tales told round fires are thereby becoming a privileged group, bonded by their vicarious strength and courage. Those who create and nourish their identity through songs sung under the stars are, in that very activity, encoding memories that are actual modifications of the neural pathways of the brain. Common celebrations like storytelling and singing—or ritual and liturgy—change brain chemistry and thus create a common memory that subsequent celebrations can evoke. But a community with nothing to celebrate will lose its identity. If ritual dies, the community dies: it is only a matter of time.

Such experiences not only reinforce the moral ties of the community but teach lessons of trustworthiness, integrity, and loyalty. Yet in contemporary Western culture, not only has it been common practice for us *not* to celebrate change, pain, or transition, and not only have we rarely told or heard the stories, but we have frequently hidden or privatized or denied them. So we make life's journeys in isolation and as individuals, rather than together as communities. It is a tragic and unnecessary feature of our apparent sophistication. There are signs of change, thank God, but we are not always good at knowing how to proceed. Because of our unfamiliarity with reading the clouds, we may easily find ourselves adrift and disoriented. So here are stories to ponder.

Ishi and the Anthropologist

In 1911, twenty years after the last of his tribe, the Yahi, was presumed exterminated by white settlers and soldiers, one who would later be called "Ishi" was "discovered" in California. He was brought to Alfred Kroeber, a sophisticated, kindly anthropologist. The two developed a touching relationship, with Ishi finding Kroeber's behavior and belief at least as odd and impenetrable as Kroeber found Ishi's.

In Ishi's world, the bodies of the dead had to be burned so that their spirits could arise like smoke. The nearest and dearest survivors had the honor and religious responsibility for singing their beloved dead to the land of the grandparents. Unless the songs were sung, the dead would never find their way home to the sacred mountain.

The anthropologist's wife died. Ishi could respect Kroeber's reluctance to burn her body but was appalled that a loving husband could refuse to sing to her corpse. How else would she rejoin her family and forebears? And if not Kroeber, who would sing her home? The anthropologist was indeed a little embarrassed at the poor impression he gave to Ishi, yet he had neither the temperament nor the voice for singing over his dead wife.

Gradually, Ishi and Alfred grew in mutual understanding and respect. The anthropologist recorded precious aspects of Ishi's life and culture, and especially his language. When Ishi, the last of his tribe, died of tuberculosis, Kroeber was truly grief-stricken. He buried Ishi with respect and love, though he still could not bring himself to burn his friend's body. But alone on a high plateau, facing the mountain of the Yahi, and with tears streaming down his face, he did find the courage and the voice, and indeed the words—which no other living person knew—to sing Ishi to the Happy Hunting Grounds of his ancestors, on the sacred peak.

We, too, collectively and individually, must find the words, though sometimes they are foreign to us. We, too, must pray for conversion and for courage in order to sing the songs and tell the stories that give life, that remind us who we are or who we can be, that join us with our ancestors and send us renewed on our journeys. This is a serious challenge, in no way self-indulgent exhibitionism. It is also an art that we might well have forgotten, or even, like the sophisticated Kroeber, we may have never really known.

Anna, Maker of Memories

Once upon a time [only this is a true story] lived a woman called Anna, the kind of mother every child could dream of. And Anna had many children of her own. She also had a devoted husband, John. All in all, a real fairy tale! But she was not only someone's mother and someone's wife; Anna was very much her own person. Yet she lived as much for others as she did for herself, which is a fine achievement. Anna was a wonderful storyteller, and she passed on to her children a marvelous range of stories. She also taught them prayers and nursery rhymes and songs. For many years, while her children were growing, hardly a single day passed without her singing, or snuggling with a child or two on her lap, holding them spellbound with her stories, lulling them to sleep with her songs.

The children grew up, but as each one came along and sat on their mother's lap, the older ones would hear again the tales from their own childhood, until they were themselves able to tell the stories and sing the songs to their little brothers and sisters. They knew who they were. They knew what they stood for. They knew what their priorities were. And with every telling of the stories they strengthened the bonds or embraced yet one more person within the strong arms of the extended family. When the last of the children left home, the house did not fall quiet, for grandchildren soon discovered the magic of Anna's voice and the music of her songs. She would sing the songs of childhood as she went about the house. And now that she and John had more time, they would say their prayers together, aloud, at the end of every day.

At the age of 73, Anna had a stroke which left her paralyzed and speechless. Now the house was quiet. John sat alone and powerless in his grief, while Anna lay in a hospital bed, far from home and husband, far from sons and daughters, far from songs and stories....

Some may say this is a rather sad ending. But at least Anna left behind memories and stories and music and song—and hope. And that's a kind of immortality. If we and our institutions did as much, it would be a blessing.

Down But Not Out, In Darwin

Among the dispossessed Aboriginal peoples, the "down and outs" living in transit camps near Darwin in Australia's Northern Territory, memories of illness and pain are nurtured and shared. Each person has some shocking experience of abuse or neglect, sickness or accident. But a fascinating fact is that the memories themselves are clearly governed by rules.

The first rule is the "can't tell" rule, which forbids the "patient" the pleasure of telling his or her "recovery story." The story and its telling become the possession of another person. Thus the "can't tell" rule is balanced by a second rule which provides for a spokesperson who alone "owns" the story as personal (not "private") property. This is the hero, the one who intervened and rescued the individual from distress. The hero is indissolubly linked to the sufferer by a bond of irredeemable debt. Every member of the community (called the "mob") is socially required, for the duration of the sickness or the recovery period, to be available, to show concern, to offer time and talents, and to empathize. If the sufferer cries out in pain, the community identifies it as "babblin'" ("thata not Billy talkin'; thata sickness talkin'"), and care is continued. Thus, it is the responsibility of the community to identify the sickness itself and the appropriate length of convalescence. The patient is not allowed to feel awkward or an imposition, for everyone in the community has a role in the care and recovery process. The sick person remains dependent on the rescuers until the end of the sickness is marked by a return of the old self: but crucially it is a different self, because the recovered person receives a new identity.

During the sickness and long after, the patient has no right to seek sympathy by telling the story. But the hero, the owner of the story, has both right and responsibility. At night, gathered round the fire, someone will call on the hero, and the story will be told. And it will be told periodically, as long as the patient's needs warrant it, and for many years after, according to its significance. But it is the community, not the individual, that determines this. And the community, in tapping its common memory, reminds itself of its communal identity and history.

Every serious illness or accident leaves its own special character: cough, limp, or scar. This is the "souvenir" or mark of a person's passage into the ranks of the walking wounded. The souvenir marks the person as someone with a story. Without a story, a man or woman has not yet become a real person. The story, owned and told by another, is the sign of one's credibility, one's social identity (Sansom, 1982; Gittins, 1987).

So, there are still people who are not taken in by the cult of the individual, and who remain social and gregarious. They seek and make meaning together: shared meaning. Does not this story resonate with us? Does not its drama recall our universal woundedness: *original sin* perhaps? It certainly accentuates the uniqueness of every person's life-experience. And it cautions that, in our desire to be heard and our need for sympathy, we risk becoming boring or selfish. Yet so significant is the experience of individuals that the group as a whole must find ways to integrate it. Otherwise individuals become alienated, groups fragment, and a human society will die. Wisdom lies in knowing what stories are important, in acknowledging them as part of life, in finding ways to remember, and in being enabled to move forward.

Gathering the Fragments

Individually and as communities we have stories: of birth, of struggles and successes, of fears and failings. We have institutional stories and local community stories. They must be remembered and told. They must be told in order to be remembered. Yet they cannot all be told, nor by everyone, nor in such a way as to cause us to become caught in the past. But we have to find the ways to remember what must not be forgotten, and to narrate and sing it. We need to dramatize and symbolize and ritualize our identity as community. This is not something others can do for us. Within our own groups of various kinds, we must discern our own real needs, determine what to hang on to and what to let go of, what is life-giving and what is death-dealing, what to transmit and what to erase. In unity and in community, we must spin the threads that will run through the fabric of our lives, past, present, and to come.

As a pilgrim people we must also cultivate creative amnesia, for we cannot cling to everything we ever did or made, lest it stifle and weigh us down when we need to travel light. As disciples of Jesus and without self-indulgence (remembering the "can't tell" rule), we will sing new life into selected stories: of heroes and unsung—but not forgotten—companions. As a people of faith, when we gather we will need to experiment with ways of remembering lest we forget, and with ways of integrating lest we disintegrate. This is so profoundly part of human culture that if we forget who we are, we will cease to exist.

Is this not why Jesus said "do this in memory of me"? For two thousand years people have struggled to be faithful to his memory, yet scandalously have so violently disagreed about what "this" refers to, that the sign of unity and inspiration has become a mark of division and disillusion. If we have focused only on bread and wine, on an Upper Room, and on a company of men, we may have identified "this" far too narrowly. The whole life of Jesus was exemplary, and *this* is what we must remember, and *do*, and replicate in word, worship, and action. If Christians are united in faith but divided in Eucharist, or if communities are brought together in worship but stratified by gender, how can they claim to be doing the "this" which was the whole life of Jesus? We have lessons to learn and apply as we continue to weave memories to sustain us.

Moving Forward With Grace

The stories in this chapter can be parables for our lives. But what about our own stories? How do we interpret our own lives, but in a broader social context? How might we use some of our personal stories in a generative manner, to add to the common store of wisdom? Humanity has a remarkable capacity to translate across languages and cultures, so we should be able to ensure that a range of stories are gathered and transmitted from one community to another. Nevertheless, this must be done in an appropriate manner, for if our stories are self-indulgent they will be of no more significance than a whimsical butterfly collection:

attractive and dazzling perhaps, but not particularly informative, and certainly not bearing wisdom for new generations.

How, then, might we use the wisdom encoded in local stories, both as a means of community-building and as an instrument of evangelization? Here is an example that might show how wisdom hidden since the foundation of the world may actually serve to cast new light on the contemporary Christian challenge. Bruce Chatwin (1987) tells of the ancient native peoples of Australia, but this is the story of everyman. And it evokes the life of the Son of Man. It is stitched together here in several pieces:

Aboriginal stories recall that every remote ancestor was thought to have scattered a trail of words and musical notes along the line of his footprints as he passed through life. These "dreaming-tracks" lay like an invisible spider web all over the land. They were, literally, creation songs, for their singing brought the world into being. That's the original meaning of poetry: it means "creation." They were pathways of communication between the most far-flung tribes and across the generations....

How reminiscent of the memory of Jesus, the creative Word uttered and brought forth by God! Jesus is the one who, by his Incarnation, makes all things new; who says of himself, in that self-disclosure of the Godhead, "I AM"; "I AM the way"; "I AM the truth"; "I AM the life"; and who invites us to follow in his footsteps, to find truth and new life.

As Christians committed to keeping the good news alive and current, we need networks of creative memories which, like our actual ancestors and physical parents, give us life and keep us alive. Such memories, like extended families and lineages, give us identity, unite us, and inspire us. So we need to know "by heart" the lines of the poetry of a God who creates, and we need to become co-creators and pro-creators. We need more song and singing in our lives, lest the rhetoric of those whose trade is death bring about the hopelessness and destruction it proclaims, and lest those with no poetry and perhaps no soul produce only the dreadful noise that causes deafness.

…Aboriginal people could not imagine the land existed before they could see and sing it. They believed their ancestors actually sang it into existence. Women, who always had their own songs, are co-creators of the world. But creation is not so much an event as a process. It did not just happen once and for all. And an unsung land is a dead land. So if the songs are forgotten or unsung the land itself will die. In traditional belief, every one is responsible for a part of the land, because an ancestor entrusted each person with part of a great song. That was the "title deed" to the land, which could never be sold or repudiated. So responsibility for the land, for creation, was a sacred trust or deed; and song was the container in which it was carried.…

A song in our Western repertoire contains the lyric: "a song is no song 'til you sing it." This lyric provides the same insight. Unless we sing our songs and tell our stories, we remain without a history and, therefore, without an identity. More pertinently, for the Jewish-Christian people, to sing the praises of God in psalms or canticles is to perform a religious act which binds the community to itself, to the land, and to the Creator. And to retell the stories of Exodus and Redemption has been to rediscover our identity and the deeper meaning of our lives as chosen people, people of the covenant, people with a destiny. This returns us to the theme of our common project.

…A profound and poetic aspect of Aboriginal people's behavior is their understanding of trade. Trade is literally life-giving to all social groups, and focuses on commodities of mutual significance,

without which there can be no continuing life for the participants.
In Australia however, the trade route is actually the Songline itself,
the strand in the web that crisscrosses the land. This is because songs,
not things, are the principle medium of exchange. Trading in "things"
is the secondary consequence of trading in song....

What a clear challenge for those committed to evangelization,
mission, ministry! Can we see ourselves as bringing "songs," and
if so, in what would they consist? Do we first "trade" these songs—
singing the Good News of God's activity in human history—
and only then extend the trade relations and offer education,
medicine, or technology? Or are we less than fluent in the songs,
or not quite convinced of their power? And do we first try to
soften up people through our trade in the attractive accessories
we bring—education, medicine, technology—so that we never
actually get round to singing our songs and telling the stories of
our faith and discipleship?

If there are indeed people who value songs and stories above
commodities, how might they respond to those who come "in
the name of the Lord" but have forgotten how or what to sing, or
who seem embarrassed to speak directly and enthusiastically of
God's love and mercy? The question is important, especially for
those who quite wrongly imagine the laity's is only a secondary
role or are concerned only with the material elements of mission
and ministry. Important, too, for those who believe in something
called "pre-evangelization." The phrase implies that people must
first be softened up with commodities, or so-called development,
before they are sufficiently ready to have the songs sung and the
stories told. Vincent Donovan aptly labels this concept an "arrogant cultural assumption."

It is surely time for all baptized people to persuade themselves
that they can and they must be announcers and singers, if their
ministry—parenting or education, medicine or music—is to have

any moral value. It is time for the whole People of God to know the songs and stories of their faith well enough to be able to sing and to speak, and for the hierarchy specifically to acknowledge that the faith is not transmitted only by theologians or by clergy, but by gift and by contagion: it is caught from people of faith.

To return to the indigenous people of Australia:

…A "stop" on the land was the handover point, where the song passed out of your ownership. You'd sing the end of your own verses, and there lay the boundary. From there on it was the responsibility of another person to continue the song, to make it comprehensible, to find the right note or key or speed. Your work was over.

Isn't this a powerful image for Christians involved in evangelization but concerned over when and how to "let go"? We are sometime too attached to our own favorite song or story, acting as though ours was the only way to sing or to narrate the gospel. And we are sometimes afraid to hand it over at the "borders."

We have to learn when the solo is over. We are not giving up, but we are called to translate, to transfer, to defer, to let the recipient receive. Unless people are able to sing their own songs and tell their own stories—of faith and grace, of the workings of God in their lives—Christianity will be a foreign import in a foreign packaging, never becoming part of people's own repertoire.

Which Stories and Songs?

How will we discern the appropriate songs and stories? How might they be sung or told? What circumstances might be more or less productive for evangelization through the medium of story or of song? How, indeed, might we modify our ministry? Here are four suggestions.

First, it is always necessary for Christians to speak the truth.

But it is not always necessary for Christians to speak! We must also listen with adequate attention and interest so that we really hear what the other person is trying to communicate. Jesus was very concerned about this: "they have ears but they do not hear," he said. We have to do better than that. True listening is not only to words or mouths, but is also careful to attend to what is between the lines: the cries of anguish, the pain, the silence, the tears. We must listen to frustration and fear, to hostility and to hopelessness, to courage and commitment: otherwise we are not really listening and therefore we cannot possibly hear. When people know that they are not being heard, they stop speaking or go elsewhere. Sometimes they become violent. We must learn patience, not foist our own agenda, and be truly committed to the other as subject. In that way, some of the stories that need to be told and remembered will flourish and survive.

Second, though listening and hearing are part of communication, they are not yet sufficient. Along with them goes an appropriate response. We cannot commit ourselves only to listening. That way, ultimately, the other person simply takes over the monologue. True communication must be dialogical. It will produce mutual feedback, reciprocity, translation. At its best, it will give rise to modification and enrichment.

Every person is worthy of respect, but none of us is without opinions and judgments that are immature or uninformed or just plain wrong. To argue for stories as part of evangelization is not to defend windy autobiography but to encourage the search for the real identity of people and communities. People's wants sometimes become confused with their needs. The former are relative, but the latter are absolutely critical. The Christian community does not commit itself to supplying its members' wants, but their needs are of paramount importance. Unless we can discern the difference we will fail to act in a Christian manner. The stories accumulated and retained over generations may be like ore containing the precious metal to be mined for the mutual enrichment of all in search of the Hidden Treasure.

Third, communication in a faith context involves interpreting, comparing, assessing, responding. We must cultivate empathy—a task so difficult as to be almost impossible. Perhaps it is only truly possible if both parties have a comparable experience: not identical experience, but probably something that has left a mark or scar. We may recall the experiences of the transients of Darwin, Australia. Empathy, so important for forging enduring bonds, is an ingredient of our own credibility. It cannot be faked. But people do not achieve credibility unless they know something about one another's stories, and unless they show real concern to know and respond to them.

Fourth, many of the most profound and enduring of the stories and songs we hear do not belong to private individuals but to people, whole groups, and communities. So when we listen, let us try to hear echoes of the story beyond the story. We may even hear strains of the music of the universe itself, in the words and tunes around us. For, without diminishing the uniqueness of each person's experience, we open a common treasure chest when we open the storybooks and songbooks. Tales and tunes can resonate as a kind of universal language, making sense to us in ways that other forms of expression cannot. This is important for those whose stories and experiences seem, on the surface, very different from one another or from our own. It is crucial, too, for those learning to listen to other languages, other music, other cultures, other histories. The stories we tell and hear, the songs we sing and listen to, have their own ways of reaching the inner person. Stories and songs are windows to the soul. Their language transcends vernaculars, and their cadences soar above our limited range. For people engaged in the ministry of evangelization, they are a priceless key for unlocking lives.

The End of the Beginning

We may gather periodically as a single group but we belong to many groups. And though united as community we are individuated as persons. We are pilgrims and we are committed to pilgrimage, a motley Christian crew on a common journey. But the journey is only a common undertaking when we are united. And unity comes through sharing experiences and shared goals. We are not a club but a community. And once in a great while we may even become *communitas,* a small group fired by an impossible dream and utterly committed to one another for the sake of the dream. That can be a blessed experience. The Transfiguration and the day of Pentecost may be examples of *communitas,* but they are rare and short-lived, for we do tend to settle into a more routine and organized life.

A community needs rules and routines to live by. An organized community is a very powerful form of social institution but it tends to be conservative: it looks after itself. *Communitas* is rather different. Born in a burst of creative energy as intense as a solar flare, it is for a moment incandescent. It is not constrained or entirely predictable. The Christian experience of *communitas* happens when a group of people are galvanized, inspired, and forged into a single point of faith-inspired commitment. In the context of religious orders, it may be spoken of as one's founding moment. In a parish community, it may be experienced in sacramental initiation (*mystagogy*). In an Age of Faith, it might actually have been experienced by people making common pilgrimage. *Communitas* has enormous potential, though it lacks the stability and predictability of a conventional community. It is characterized by zeal, and by resilient fragility that is neither weakness nor brute strength. But *communitas* is virtually impossible to sustain; it is essentially ephemeral, for as soon as institutionalization (marked by rational organization) takes over, *communitas* has imperceptibly given way to *community*.

Institutionalized *community* is incapable of bringing creative and prophetic change for it has to accommodate too many people, and its strength lies in conservativeness rather than innovation. Evangelization is a call—a reiterated invitation—to *communitas*, for evangelization is what Jesus does and it is creative and utterly transforming. All are invited but not all come (Lk 14:15–24). Many are called but few are chosen (Mt 22:14). For Christians, word and sacrament are foundational for sustaining our fragile commitment. The Eucharist is the primary experience that can transform our associations and communities of individuals into prophetic *communitas*. And we break and share the Word when we interlace common stories and songs to weave the fabric that holds us together. This is how the Body of Christ is constituted and strengthened. This is the transformation and reconciliation of all things in Christ. As Doris Donnelly put it: "When [such transformation] happens there is homogeneity, and absence of rank. When *communitas* emerges, the deep story that binds the pilgrims holds them together....The exchange of stories assists the process as men and women enter into the human experience of others, and return to themselves, and eventually to home base, richer for the passage" (Donnelly, 1992:31).

Anna's Never-Ending Story (continued)

...Anna was incapacitated by a stroke. The stories stopped; the joy of life seemed to have ebbed completely. Day after day, John left the loneliness of his home and came to his wife's hospital bed where Anna lay, alert but without words, smiling but silent. Day after day, he sat, mute and attentive, at her side, without communication and without hope. And every night he went home, his shoul-

ders more hunched, his step slower and less sure, his own life gradually ebbing away.

One day, looking into Anna's alert but frightened eyes, John decided to pray with her, even though she could not respond. "In the name of the Father," he said slowly and reverently, "and of the Son, and of the Holy Ghost...." And Anna, following intently with her eyes, flickered her lips. Then from those lips, now split by a beaming, newborn smile, burst a triumphant "Amen"! From that moment Anna and John were renewed. "Hail Mary, full of...," said John; "grace," said Anna! "Our Father who art in...," said John; and Anna would shout an exultant "heaven!"

From there it was a short step to the songs, and then to the stories. John would start a song they both knew, and after a few words Anna would add one, then two, and three words more; she could almost always complete the line. John went home and found an old storybook that Anna had used long ago with her children and grandchildren. And now John became the storyteller, and it was Anna who was spellbound. And just like a child learning the stories, she would add an appropriate word, or struggle to finish the sentence. "I'll huff and I'll puff and I'll...," said John; "blowww the houssse dowwwnnn," said Anna, with as much pleasure as effort.

Each day John would arrive at the hospital with a new idea. He bought children's storybooks and read them to Anna, much to her delight and comprehension. He said his prayers with her and she always completed the sentence or the prayer. He even sang songs to her in his quiet voice. Anna's children came too. And the stories that, long ago she had given to them, taught them, and told them many times, and that they in turn had taught and told to their own children, they now gave back to their own mother. And her face broadened in a smile of love and achievement.

A few weeks later Anna quietly passed away. But by the time she died, the stories she had told and the songs she had sung were alive again in the lives of her children and grandchildren, not to mention *the nurses and doctors who became part of her growing circle of family and friends, united, renewed, and committed to life, through common memories and common experience.*

Stories like that are good news. And good news demands a hearing. We all have stories, though we may have forgotten some and not found opportunities to share others. We are also people of faith and we belong to communities of faith. We need to recall our stories just as we recall the story of Jesus. "Do this in memory of me," he said. *This* is not just bread and wine but a whole life, a whole life-story. Do this *in memory of me* implies that if we stop doing it we will forget, we will lose the memory of Jesus. So we gather to tell the story and to break the bread. But we must not forget to bring our own stories, just as we must not forget to bake the bread.

Chapter Four

Healing and Wholeness: A Cross-Cultural Perspective

How do we know when dawn is near? It is when you can look into the face of the others and recognize them as your brothers and sisters. Until then, it is night.

HASIDIC WISDOM

History tells us that many a time when the church intended to achieve a good purpose by jurisdiction, it reaped a bitter harvest; when it came as a servant, minds and hearts opened up to its message and people responded.

LADISLAS ORSY

Yea, we are mad as they are mad;
Yea, we are blind as they are blind;
Yea, we are very sick and sad
Who bring good news to [human]kind.

G.K. CHESTERTON

Crossing Over

Everyone is born in a specific place and raised in a particular social situation. This is significant; but it is equally significant that human beings move or relocate. Between infancy and adulthood everyone must move from relationships of dependence to relationships of independence and interdependence. Those who fail to branch out and encounter life beyond the purely domestic sphere remain limited and immature. "What should they know of England who only England know?" asked the poet Kipling. Only when we step outside can we appreciate our point of departure.

Some of us are also called, by the demands of faith, to leave home. Only if we are first centered and rooted, and if we have a sense of identity and moral purpose, are we in a position to move appropriately to the edges of our familiar world. There we encounter not only the current limits of our competence and comfort but the possibility of real insight and even wisdom. The Jesus who beckons us to come, also sends us in the direction of broader horizons and more fruitful relationships.

Consistent with the attempt to involve every baptized person in evangelization, yet not to reduce the notion of mission to a simple matter of distance or geography, let us pay particular attention to actual ministerial contexts. Of course, we will not avoid considering boundaries or thresholds, the margins or edges that delimit our familiar worlds. But first a word about culture, and the possibilities of being cross-cultural.

Culture, once defined as "the man-made [human] part of the environment," includes belief and thought, symbol and ritual, language and song, and rather aptly characterizes humanity. Yet no culture is without flaws. We may say culture ranges from poetry to pollution, from music to missiles, from dance to deforestation, and includes art and religion, meanings and memories, the sin and the grace. And just as there is no single universal language or religion or music, so there is no single monolithic culture. There are myriad human cultures.

A culture is shared by a society or group of people, but problems arise if we try to specify the number of human cultures. All human beings share in a common humanity. Thus, we are essentially the same. But we are also individually unique. We cannot argue that there are as many cultures as there are people, for that would destroy the social component of culture. It's easy to say that a society or group of people who are geographically far away are of another culture, so going and living among them could thus be a cross-cultural enterprise. But there are nuances. And what about closer to home?

A multicultural society has, by definition, people of many cultures. However, simply being surrounded by people of different cultures does not make one cross-cultural in any meaningful sense, though it is possible in such circumstances truly to engage in cross-cultural communication. And it should be obvious that to go many leagues from home simply to be outnumbered by, rather than engaged with, people of a different culture is not to be cross-cultural.

The test of a cross-cultural encounter is in the quality of commitment, the degree of risk-taking and trusting, the amount of sharing of vulnerability, and the active learning of the meanings of the lives of those different from ourselves. It is not easy, and certainly not just a matter of good intentions. But a culture is a human reality, not only located in the mind but embodied in people. The implications are enormous, both for those who cross cultural boundaries in search of other embodied people, and because Christianity is *par excellence* a religion of incarnation, of embodiment. It is about Jesus the Christ, God become human, and not generic but specifically male.

There are still further subtleties and degrees. Such is the vari-

ety of human experience and the multiplicity of worlds of meaning, that it is possible for true cross-cultural challenges to be very
close to home. Some people may say that in the contemporary
world, a family is itself a cross-cultural arena. But in principle, at
least, families are stable contexts for the socialization of their
members. More eligible for the title might be a marriage, certainly in its early stages, if the spouses come from very different
backgrounds or cultures. Between the extremes of exotically
cross-cultural experiences and every single interpersonal relationship there are many authentic yet overlooked cross-cultural
challenges.

Perhaps it is time to rehabilitate the notion of a subculture,
without its purely negative associations. It can refer quite simply
to a group of people identified as such by virtue of distinctive
behaviors and values. A criminal gang or a monastic community
would be examples: a subculture need not only describe a group
outside the law. Each of us belongs to a subculture within the
broader culture, a denomination or professional group perhaps.
And where people of different subcultures encounter each other,
the encounter may be as truly cross-cultural as the differences
between the subcultures are real.

Wisdom is often discovered at the edges of familiar worlds.
What we learn about human dignity or heroism frequently comes
from people whose circumstances seem at first sight very different from our own. Jesus is an obvious case in point. He who
brought healing and preached repentance among the Jewish
people rarely encountered a Gentile without engaging in healing. All his encounters with non-Jews were marked by their
boundary-breaking character, which moved one or both of them
to new insight and depth of communication. And every encounter between Jesus and an outsider brings about real change. Jesus
is edified and surprised at the faith he finds.

As for ourselves, we may have reached middle age and been

visited by whispers of approaching death. We may know only too well that we are physically failing. We may have solid experience and embodied knowledge of our mortality. Yet we do not necessarily fall victim to anticipatory anxiety and panic. Nevertheless, we do need to learn from these experiences, and our learning may be enhanced by people more acquainted with approaching death than ourselves. Some of our feelings of panic at the prospect of chronic pain or the loss of sight may also be eased by encounters with other people closer to those realities.

Journeys to the worlds of the sick and dying, the vulnerable and suffering ones, may lead to bedsides in hospitals in the United States or to remote villages in Africa. Either way, they take us to the limits of more familiar worlds. Such journeys should provoke serious reflection both on the reality of suffering and on the Christian task of accompanying others and being committed to healing as Jesus was. This chapter is a reflection on the ministerial possibilities of boundaries, and on elements of a spirituality of healing. It is particularly for those engaged in ministries of healing, but should have implications for us all, recipients no less than givers of care. Consistent with previous chapters, we look for wisdom wherever it may be found. We start in the Kalahari desert of South-West Africa, among the people called !Kung San (Katz, 1982).

Pain of Healing and Healing of Pain

Jesus, and the people of his culture, clearly distinguished curing from healing. So do the !Kung. They do not expect cures for everything, though they hope some things may be alleviated in time. And they communally and clearly accept the necessity and naturalness of death. They do not try to outrun death, nor do they imagine that to bring about a cure is to capture the secret of immortality. Instead, they face and embrace life-in-the-midst-of-death and death-in-the-midst-of-life, above all, in a humble spirit of commitment to healing. Critically, the commitment is *by* the community as a whole, and to the healing *of* the community as a whole. Individuals will, of course, become sick from time to time, and a variety of individual people may be significant healers on different occasions. But the community that heals is the community that is healed, and without a healing community there can be no permanent or convincing healing of individuals. This is the !Kung understanding of the healing process.

The people's commitment to community-building is such that when an old person is diagnosed as terminal, efforts are actually intensified, not in the hopes of staving off death but in order to heal the dying person according to the criteria of a deeper wisdom: that healing is far more profound than simple curing. A community that gathers to support its dying members is one that is enhancing its own well-being. Communities unable or unwilling to foregather in the presence of death will slowly die.

This approach to healing tends to underscore the value of living fully, of neither avoiding nor denying, of not fleeing pain, but of learning life's therapeutic value and the appropriate place of pain.

A Community of Healing

To the !Kung, illness points to an imbalance between the individual and the total environment. A "healing" seeks to re-establish the balance. One expression might be a cure; or the person who is healed may nevertheless die. But it is always possible for a new balance to be established, for healing involves work not only on the individual but on the group, and on the surrounding environment and cosmos.

Not everyone is a healer, since the healing power represents commitment to a quest, and those who aspire to heal must be purified.

To heal the community is to suffer for it, and the healer's pain can be all but unbearable. The greatest healers suffer the greatest pain, as well as the greatest fear.

People know that a healing environment is a prerequisite for healing. If communities are not trained for healing, there will be no healing in the next generation. Healing power is not a scarce resource, so there is no reason to compete for it (Katz, 1982:34,45–46,53–54,118,198).

The people's wisdom is that all sickness has a social aspect: that people are *social* beings; that unless the social context and cause of sickness is addressed there will be no permanent or true recovery; that *real healing is impossible without the whole community.* This experience, of what we in the West have recently embodied in the aphorism "no pain, no gain," is also the embrace of a truly frightening passage into the unknown. Embarked on alone and unprepared, it would be alienating and destructive. Within a supportive group it can become redemptively transformational.

What the !Kung have been celebrating for a thousand years is remarkably evocative of the healing approach of Jesus and the early Christian community (Jas 5:13–16). As well as challenging his own culture, Jesus also used its authentic wisdom. We, too, may apply lessons learned from Jesus as we encounter people and cultures who have incorporated healing wisdom themselves. If we commit ourselves to reading the clouds as do people like the !Kung, we may ourselves be transformed by the grace of cross-cultural encounters.

The Dangerous Edge

The journey to the edge need not take us as far afield as the Kalahari desert, but it will never be without its challenges. Here are lines by Robert Browning:

Our interest's on the dangerous edge of things:
the honest thief, the tender murderer,
the superstitious atheist....
We watch while these in equilibrium keep
the giddy line midway: one step aside,
they're classed and done with.
I, then, keep the line
before your eyes ("Bishop Bloughram's Apology," l. 396ff).

"They're classed and done with" describes the fate of many people on the edges of our familiar world: prisoners, prostitutes, pedophiles, to name but three. When we want to keep our boundaries and prejudices strong, we do tend to classify and exclude, to judge and condemn, to stereotype and reduce. But as Christians committed to an inclusive and reconciling ministry, we must keep the "giddy line" or "dangerous edge" before our eyes, lest we forget who challenges us and of whom we are afraid. We should be in no doubt: there is a dangerous edge, where clarity meets fog, wisdom touches ignorance, certainty confronts faith. And we are fascinated by it, even drawn to it as a precipice—though sometimes, like the !Kung, as fearful as we are excited.

But edges, boundaries, borders, and margins are also where splendid things take place, relationships and breakthroughs occur, new perspectives are glimpsed, and conversion can happen. The Synoptic Gospels are full of stories of outreach and healing. In fact, this is the essential missionary metaphor. Healing is itself a means of outreach; and reaching out is accomplished in healing restoration.

Many communities have discovered the potential of the "dangerous edge." Fear of personal limitations and of the reality of pain should not make us abdicate responsibilities or leave resources unharnessed. We are called to be healers, however wounded we may have been. We are called to be a community, however much we have been estranged. Still, we may need to rediscover our healing powers. Unless we know ourselves to be part of communities rather than lone rangers, there will be no true or lasting healing, despite possibly impressive medico-surgical cures.

The !Kung may have further lessons for us. They live in small bands that average perhaps forty people, but although every adult is eligible, not everyone actually becomes a healer. Some self-exclude, despite group assurances of their ability. Those who do become healers have a strong sense of personal identity and a particularly trusting temperament. Their bodies may not be young or beautiful or even strong, and their trust is certainly not reckless. To be a healer is to embrace the pain one fears. Learning the healer's role is almost as painful a struggle as the healing itself. Healing demands that the healer step out onto the dangerous edge, the threshold of pain, the boundary that marks the safe haven of the community within.

Pain and death are neither to be denied nor fled. For the !Kung that might lead to the limbo of drug-induced coma or the isolation of people from their natural community. It could also alienate the healthy from those marked by illness or death. But a healer who can face the fears implicit in the therapeutic vocation may help troubled souls find community precisely when their lives push them to the dangerous edge. Then, instead of producing denial and alienation, sickness can be a catalyst for integration. This is authentic healing. This is a dangerous edge that is worth our own attention.

Fear of Transformation and Transformation of Fear

It would not be helpful to romanticize the !Kung. The following words are no flight of fancy of mine, and they do describe spiritual wisdom rather well:

Becoming a healer demands a transformation, a new experience of reality, leading to intensified contact with a transpersonal or spiritual realm. Healers have a sense of connectedness joining healing power, self, and the community. They move continually between fear of the transforming experience and desire to heal. One must die to oneself and transcend fear and pain, even of one's death. Precisely at such times of suffering is true community built (Katz, 1982:310,306).

The gospel itself is hardly more explicit; here surely is a further intimation of God's revelation. But to commit *ourselves* to such radical healing we must be as open to transformation as the !Kung. Can we—wherever we may be—identify and move toward the dangerous edge? Can we hope to live with integrity expressed in mutual trust shared with those we encounter there? Or are we really afraid of our own transformation?

In the current "high-tech" approach to medicine and surgery in the West, the huge majority of Christians are quite unfamiliar with *the culture of healing.* Our encounter with it is thus a potentially cross-cultural experience. We may resist this idea, whether because we are afraid to admit our own ignorance, or because healing and medicine are already part of our current ministry and we fear the radical challenge.

To undertake a ministry of healing is to follow the footsteps of Jesus. But people of faith should not forget to be people of prudence and good manners. Without a commitment to building trust and mutuality it will be impossible to create healing community, and equally impossible to read the clouds.

Sometimes narrow professionalism or doctrinaire religion keep us safe within the boundaries of our familiar worlds. Either we project a certain mystique, or others feel somewhat intimidated by our apparent competence, or both. But we Christians, people of faith and love, and maybe professional expertise as well, are challenged to create new communities, not ever-narrower competencies. Physicians and pastors, nurses and chaplains—whoever we may be and whatever our competence—we must learn to trust one another with some of our vulnerability, ignorance, incompetence, and fears, as much as we impress one another with our expertise and energy. Then our meetings on the dangerous edge—where health encounters morbidity, life looks in the face of death, and fear gives way to peace—might help build up communities of faith, as they heal and restore the broader human community.

Many Christian ministers are independent-minded, jealous of professional status, and highly competent in covering up faultlines and fragility. At the very moment that we need support and encouragement, forgiveness and love, we may make it most difficult for a compassionate friend or competent professional to assist in our healing.

Seeking Wisdom

A modern hospital can be both confusing and intimidating to those who are unfamiliar with its design and purpose. Hospitals are, of course, highly organized and full of meaning and possibility to those who understand them. The same is true of different cultures, including the church: they look and feel very different, depending on whether we are insiders or outsiders.

Hospitals, cultures, and the church are alike insofar as they contain or embody their own characteristic wisdom. As an African proverb says, "Wisdom is not bought." Yet, as Luke's Gospel says, "Jesus increased in wisdom." As we move beyond our narrow limitations, cross boundaries, and engage with other people and other worlds, we may be able to share some of the wisdom that would otherwise elude us. Perhaps, too, we may carry some wisdom as a gift to others. Such exchange is intrinsic to evangelization, ministry, mission.

To branch out in an encounter with others is to walk by faith. To walk by faith is to be accompanied by grace and to be not far from miracles. Jesus went in search of faith, and wherever he found it, miracles resulted. Only, and always, where there was lack of faith was he unable to do miracles (Mk 6:5–6). If we can bring faith to the unfamiliar experience of boundary-crossing, we will find the grace to pursue our journeys.

Those who undertake a centrifugal ministry will experience transitions, ambiguity, and encounters with strangers. This itself may explain why relatively few people venture beyond their own familiar world. But for those who do there is certainly grace, and wisdom, in the experience.

Transition

Transitions put people "betwixt and between": in unfamiliar territory, neither close to former points of reference nor entirely sure of destinations. Some people refer to this kind of transition as the experience of liminality.

Liminality (*limen*: threshold) can only be interpreted in terms of what preceded and what follows. It assumes a process or a journey. Liminality marks a phase which is both necessary and—potentially, though never automatically—transformative. Adolescence, with its pains and prospects, is a transitional phase between childhood and adulthood. An orchard in full bloom is in a transitional phase between early spring growth and the full fruit of autumn.

Liminal experiences mark the passage of human life, all the way from pre-cradle to post-grave. No one changes from child to adult, becomes a parent, or reaches retirement without passing through intermediate and sometimes painful stages. In contemporary Western culture many boundary-marking *rites of passage* have become extinct, though baptisms and bar mitzvahs, marriages and funerals survive. But denying the need for transition-markers does not make them unnecessary.

Sickness is a liminal experience. So, *par excellence,* is death. People who live and work with these realities are inevitably affected by the experience of transitions and the attendant marginalization or liminality they entail. Because it is a highly charged and confusing atmosphere, a place of births and bypasses, of disease and death, a hospital is a hothouse of liminality. To be effective ministers of care in such a context we must unmask some mechanisms of denial, and embrace the ambiguity and confusion that is part of transitional living. More than that, as people of faith and as Christian ministers, we can provide encouragement, even stability, and bring order to the apparent chaos.

Medical and pastoral staff are as prone to denial as any suffering patient or family. As ministers and people of faith, our denials may have a different object: to conceal incompetence or avoid accountability, perhaps to hide blind prejudice. And we may resist our own vulnerability and liminality. But our lab coats and clerical collars, our badges and Bibles, titles and stethoscopes, mark us as marginal people on a dangerous edge. Our biggest problem might be in imagining ourselves in control of processes of life and death, when we should know that *liminality* is necessarily an experience of not being in control. But if we acknowledged that neither medicine nor surgery, and certainly neither physicians nor chaplains, are in total control of life and death, we may be better placed to become a *community* of and among other marginal people.

Jesus the minister was marginal. Marginal also means not fully self-sufficient, and on the edge of someone else's territory. Jesus the physician was liminal. Liminal implies a willingness to take risks and indicates that one is not in total control. Jesus the man was afraid. To be afraid implies to be in need of assurance. To be liminal is to be human. To be human is to be wounded, a sufferer: literally a "patient"! If patients or families are on the margin or at the edge of endurance and experience, must not physicians and ministers meet them there, on that dangerous edge, and suffer together in the healing drama where liminality may be transformed into transcendence, where fear may give way to assurance and pain to peace? Liminality should be *creative* space betwixt and between, where twin souls meet and where struggles are made meaningful.

Ambiguity

Most of us simply don't like ambiguity or uncertainty. To live creatively with ambiguity is to recognize, befriend, or at least respect it. Some uncertainty can be dispelled by knowledge, which itself may be increased by communication. So why should we guard our knowledge so jealously? Why are we afraid to share it? Why do we bridle when challenged? How can we hope to be trusted and involved in the healing process if we guard our autonomy or professionalism in this way? How can there be a collaborative community of healers unless there is real mutuality that is unafraid of questions, and not embarrassed to be seen in compassionate as well as in rational roles, prepared to be ministered to as well as to seize the opportunity to minister?

There is still an overwhelming public perception that hospitals are primarily institutions of curing and life extension. Yet in many countries of the North, considerably more than 90 percent of us die in such places. Consequently, hospitals are highly ambiguous, and working and serving in them can be very uncertain. It would be very helpful if we were able to accept this fact. But ministers of pastoral care can sometimes actually contribute to the denial of death, dispensing kindly words and pious hopes, where honesty and support might demand another version of truth. And the way some of us live, with our denials and secrecy and fear, may actually make things worse. A reexamination of these distortions may help resolve some of the confusion and contribute to more honest communication and healing service. Anything less will propagate dishonesty, which is incompatible with healing.

Strangers

Whenever meaning is ambiguous and people's intentions are unclear, we experience alienation. If this happens, neighbors may never become more than strangers, and strangers may be feared. Many people appear to be afraid, not so much of actual strangers as of the confusion anticipated if a stranger should take control. Then lines of communication may become short-circuited. Yet, in reality, strangers are often considerate. And though we may be apprehensive of the unknown other, strangers can uniquely fulfill a crucial function: they may open our eyes, illuminate our horizons, and offer new and unexpected perspectives.

A hospital may fail as a community. Even if relatively successful as an efficient institution, it may only be—anomalously—a community of strangers. A chaplain or pastoral minister may at first be perceived as a stranger who behaves unpredictably and even incomprehensibly before patients and staff. Doctors are widely known as a strange and privileged breed, with their sacred language and incantations. Patients, too, are often rather odd, regimented in a universe of free spirits, frequently horizontal in a vertical world. Their thoughts are routinely interpreted for them, and without being consulted they are told what they want and how they feel. They are woken when asleep, given what they cannot refuse, fed when full, and starved when empty!

Jesus was perceived as a stranger by his own, was unrecognized by many, yet found recognition among other strangers. Some people criticized him or were scandalized by him; some treated him as an outcast among outcasts, a sinner among sinners. Not surprisingly, he could work no miracles among those who denied their sickness. Amazed at their unbelief (Mk 6:6), he marveled at the faith of those who felt his compassion.

Yet Jesus the stranger was also a catalyst: he accelerated the pace of change, caused unimaginable reactions, offered unexpected alternatives, enabled healing to happen, precipitated novelty. People came to expect something exciting when he was around, and he in turn was excited by their faith-filled responses. Yet no one could predict his actions any more than he could control their response to grace. Nevertheless, in this community the reign of God was promoted. Together they ministered: the woman at the well and the one who bathed his feet with her hair; the Gerasene demoniac and the little man in the tree whose table and soul were graced by Jesus. Jesus could only minister where there was trust. The same could be said of his disciples (cf. Mk 6:12–13), then and now.

As institutions, hospitals can no more bring real healing to persons than churches can heal souls. Healing is a spark of the divine carried in earthen vessels. But people—physicians, nurses, chaplains, faith-filled families—may bring about cures and participate significantly in the drama of healing, not in hospitals or churches as institutions, but inasmuch as they become real communities; not as doctors or clergy in their capacity as technicians, but inasmuch as they become true healers, and a community of caring and respectful strangers.

Walking the Dangerous Edge

There it is: the dangerous edge. It is not very far away, and it borders the lives of everyone. It may be as close as the neighborhood hospital, the penitentiary, or the homeless shelter. It is also a fascinating edge, fraught with ambiguity and promise; a boundary or margin capable of including as well as excluding; a gathering place; a world of confusion that can produce a new creation; a universe of strangers where true hospitality can exist. Such an edge marks the threshold of a true boundary-breaking ministry, a cross-cultural experience. It beckons every one of us, whoever and wherever we may be. In a place like a hospital it demands serious commitment to reading the clouds if we are to discern in such a cosmos the place and significance of healing. But there are many other places, other contexts.

Do we believe the Spirit who is making everything new? Or the Jesus who responds to the man who says "If you want to, you can cure me" with "Of course I want to: be healed!" (Mk 1:40–41)? Then we must set ourselves to the healing process with new purpose. In collaboration and without competition, let us identify problems, count blessings, and learn to live creatively in a world of transitions, ambiguity, and strangers.

Here are wise words:

We are called to reach out, to deepen relationship or to right wrong relations, that is, those which deny, destroy, or prevent human dignity from arising, as we recall each other into the power of personhood. We are called to journey this way, to stay in and with the radical power of love.

When you do that for me, I am often overwhelmed by your generosity, and I may speak of the sacrifice you make for me. But you are not thereby practicing the virtue of sacrifice upon me. You are merely passing on the power of love, gifting me as others have gifted you, into that power to do radical love. This is healing love (Harrison, 1981:53).

Finally, here are some practical suggestions for finding a way to walk the dangerous edge, and to practice a Christian spirituality that embodies healing in those who meet at that edge. First, there is an urgent need to move from the increasing fragmentation of medical and therapeutic systems toward an explicit integration of healing and holistic care. Physicians and pastoral caregivers need each other's insights and expertise on many issues. Interdisciplinary work will only succeed if this is acknowledged. A bold initiative might produce real wisdom. If communities such as the !Kung, whose life is as difficult as any on earth, have found a way to holistic healing, perhaps we have to walk to other margins and boundaries before we discover the synthesis that will work for us. This raises a second issue.

An environment of healing cannot be created artificially, outside of society or in a socially antiseptic microcosm. Healing is a human, social, and *total* experience; as such it requires integration rather than segregation. Why do our hospitals segregate people? Furthermore, human wisdom is many-stranded and multiculturally contextualized; so healing (like peace or trade) must engage the margins and the marginal, the other as well as the self. Why do so many people feel excluded from the process of healing, this quintessentially human endeavor?

Pastoral care could be very influential here, inviting and involving medical administrators and promoting marriages between institutional efficiency and human compassion. Compassion may not be a line item on a budget, and may find little welcome within streamlined expansion plans. But if morale is low, employees critically overworked, and pastoral ministers deliberately marginalized, then the healing enterprise—the quality of healthcare measured on the scales of compassion and moral support—will have been immolated on the altar of expediency or profit. Pastoral care may be uniquely placed to mobilize old resources in new ways and to justify new allocations of limited funds. But unless Western society with all its scientific and technical expertise ensures that where there is suffering grace may also abound, and where there is knowledge wisdom also flourishes, then its civilization deserves to be scattered on desert sands like a hundred supposedly invincible cultures before it.

A third observation is that both clergy and physicians need to be demythologized. It is not enough for ministers to speak pious platitudes while urging trust in a God who seems to have abandoned people. It is not good enough for physicians to absolve themselves of all responsibility for death while taking inordinate credit for life. That would take us far indeed from the healing community epitomized by the !Kung. They suffer and rejoice both in life and death. Their healers expressly take upon themselves a prime share of suffering so that the less able may be spared the burden. Doctors and ministers must dare to show their human face and to express human feelings and to be an integral part of the community that suffers, and not simply outsiders sent to redeem it. Our redeemer took on our suffering and *became as we are.* As physicians and clergy, nurses and pastoral caregivers, but Christians and ministers first, who are we, and who do we think we are?

An urgent duty binding all Christians, without exception, is commitment to the realm of God. The sign of the coming of the kingdom is that justice reigns, the sick and the dying are comforted, and those crushed in spirit are treated tenderly; tears are wiped away though they continue to flow, the impoverished are supported, and the dying are comforted. This is not some impossible Utopia but a community of mutuality, and it must begin building now, today. Consequently, and a fourth point, in a world of individualism and consumerism, science and technology must be evangelized, challenged, harnessed for communities and for the whole, rather than for individuals and for the multinationals. A hospital is a crossroads where the values of the kingdom may conflict with those of science and technology—or where all may be enriched. But without dialogue between gospel values and secular human aspirations, the mission of God will be frustrated and the whole community will be impoverished. Pastoral care teams have a historic opportunity to invite the scientific community to a dialogue about fundamental human values. The celebrated anthropologist Margaret Mead reminded us that not only can a small and committed group of people change the world, but that it's never more than a small committed group that does, or has! Pastoral caregivers are a good example of a small group of people that could bring about a revolution.

There is throughout post-modern society a great malaise. It is the failure to find meaning, to identify a deeper purpose in life than either survival or self-interest. Where is God's revelation? If we persist in denying death or human limitations, how can authentic values be discovered? If people accept the "quick fix" approach to malfunction or poor physical design, and if dollars are valued over sense, then where are we going? So, fifth, we must rediscover our relationship with the transcendent, and the potential for virtue and heroism. God's revelation can show that our finiteness is indeed compatible with transcendence, with an indomitable human spirit supported by God's Holy Spirit. God's revelation can convince us that "annihilation" and "technical failure" do not describe death, much less explain it, and that fatalism is not an acceptable human response. We must look beyond, rise above, and be lifted up. Christians involved in a ministry of pastoral care have an initiating and sustaining responsibility.

Education for Transcendence

One of the pieces written about !Kung healing is called "education for transcendence" (Katz, 1976). So far in this chapter we have not yet seen exactly what is involved. But since all of us Christian believers are invited to ongoing conversion, which also involves transcendence of self, this may be the appropriate moment.

Surprisingly, perhaps, what the !Kung do is dance! Dance is a primeval, universal ritual and religious response. We saw it previously, with reference to the Aboriginal Australians and the Songlines. We have memorialized it in Christian art and music with reference to Jesus as "Lord of the Dance." We may recall the whirling dances of Sufi dervishes or the more restrained community dancing of the Shakers, the abandonment of Haitian Vodun (Voodoo) dancing, or the majestic Thunderbird dances of the Kwakiutl of the Pacific Northwest. But in countless cultures religious dance is inseparable from healing, community, and the acknowledgment of human embodiment. So where is the dance in our hospitals and comfortable churches? And why might the question itself seem faintly absurd? African-Americans have not forgotten how to sway in their suffering and dance away their despair, and the Hispanic heritage is characterized by the rhythmic movement of procession and pilgrimage. But we cannot dance or move together if we are pulled apart by denial, whether of our incompleteness and need or of our poverty and fears. Our inhibitions cripple us, and we forget that Jesus gave his disciples the same powers he exercised, powers to be used for healing (Mk 16:17–18). Perhaps the example of the !Kung may trigger in us new ways to dance appropriately.

Healing is the road to meaning and wholeness, in individuals and with the environment. Consciousness includes acting, seeing, thinking, and feeling. An altered state like meditation or the experience of transcendence is radically different from everyday consciousness. Those seeking healing bring hopes and fears. In all-night dances accompanied by singing, and with the whole community, more than a third of the adults routinely alter their state of consciousness, releasing healing energy on the entire community. The "healers" are those willing to undergo intense pain, yet the dance is a happy event. All who come are healed. Dances are part of life, take place up to twice a week, and !Kung have danced thus for hundreds of years. Healing is applied to physical ills, but also to social problems, allowing release of frustration, bringing participants in contact with the source of their being, the creator, God. Healing dances are as much about preventing preventable sickness as about curing current malaise.

A healthy community is a prerequisite for healing. If tension is unresolved, no dances can take place and no healing (Katz, 1976: *passim*).

"All who come are healed." How reminiscent of the gospel which says "all those who touched him were healed" (Mk 6: 56). Do we not see, among the !Kung, a kind of sacrament of reconciliation, a form of anointing of the sick, and a foreshadowing of Eucharist? Here, surely, is a celebration of the sacraments of life.

As believers—clergy or physicians, ministers of word or sacrament—where are our communal rituals, our healing dances, our ceremonies of reconciliation? There are some, but there could be others, better integrated and more freely shared. We could learn to dance, to process, to embrace, to suffer, and to reach our center—but together and not in private, as communities and not as isolated specialists. Which gives rise to a sixth and final suggestion: we could make the commitment to learning how to become healers and not simply fixers. It could be a more explicit part of our Christian spirituality. After all, there is a tradition that Jesus made a promise to all believers: "they will lay their hands on the sick, who will recover" (Mk 16:18). We might paraphrase "they will recover" more literally as "they will have beauty, appropriateness, nobility"! What a transformation such noble and appropriate beauty would bring to our hospitals, homes, and bedsides!

If societies cannot be defined except in terms of human embodiment, then what bridges might we have to construct in order to engage people of other cultures? Dance is one. Healing is another.

Long ago and far away, there was a healer who said "whoever believes in me will perform the same works as I do myself, will perform even greater works" (Jn 14:12). The word for this activity in Greek is *therapeuein,* which gives the English "therapeutic." It does *not* mean "to cure." The nearest English equivalent is "to minister," "to be an attendant," or "to wait on." How interesting and providential that the function of "minister" and that of "physician" should occupy the same ground! We talk of an "attending" physician, and we can be reminded that to be "therapeutic" is to be a "minister." Thus a minister is a healer and a healer is a minister—or should be. As familiar strangers walking a creative if dangerous edge, we share a common call to become a community of healers and a healing community. That is a measure of our spirituality.

Chapter Five

Caring and Prophecy: Retrieving a Tradition

The most important thing is not survival but prophecy.

JOAN CHITTISTER

Even if a brother who fasts six days were to hang himself by the nose, he could not equal the one who serves the sick.

YUSHI NOMURA

Tradition without vision is heresy.

JOAN CHITTISTER

"Never Try to Suppress the Spirit"
(1 Thess 5:19)

The ministry of Jesus focused on healing care: all who touched him were cured (Mk 6:56). He sent his disciples in pairs, to continue the healing ministry (Lk 10:1, 9). We are baptized with the same spirit of Jesus (1 Cor 12:13); and signs associated with believers include laying hands on the sick, who will recover (Mk 16:18). So how do we, as Christians, currently understand healing, and what part does it play in our lives? Or is it a thing of the past, or the concern of others? We turn now to look at both the ministry of care and the prophetic tradition, hoping we may become increasingly committed to prophetic care and healing outreach in a broken and bleeding world.

God is utterly bountiful. Saint Bonaventure spoke of God as self-giving goodness (*bonum diffusivum sui*). Believers have always been awed by God's goodness, seeing it manifested particularly in the wonders of creation. What Christians sometimes overlook is that we humans also exemplify God's goodness. From the beginning, not only the light, the earth and the seas, the vegetation, the sun and moon and stars, the living creatures, the heavens and the earth and the animals, but humanity—each and all are described as good. When the stage was set and God looked at the whole of creation, "God saw all that God had made, and indeed it was very good" (Gen 1:31).

Before chaos became creation, "God's spirit hovered over the water" (Gen 1:2). The story of humanity is inseparable from the story of God's spirit. Long before Jesus gave us the Holy Spirit as the comforter whom the church came to identify formally as the third Person of the Trinity, God's spirit—the ruach, or wind— was already active in the world. In the Jewish Bible, that spirit was particularly manifested in prophecy, the living word of God that never entirely vanished from the Chosen People.

In the New Testament, Luke's Gospel opens with a half-dozen indications of the abiding presence of God's spirit: the angel told the father of John the Baptist that "even from his mother's womb he will be filled with the Holy Spirit" (1:15); at the Annunciation, Mary was assured that "the Holy Spirit will come upon you" (1:35); when Elizabeth heard Mary's greeting, she herself "was filled with the Holy Spirit" (1:41); just before John the Baptist was circumcised, "his father Zechariah was filled with the Holy Spirit" (1:67), and proclaimed the prophetic words that we know as the *Benedictus;* as the Holy Family went to the Temple for the Presentation, they encountered Simeon, "and the Holy Spirit rested on him" (2:25). He, too, uttered the prophetic words we know as the *Nunc Dimittis.* And, finally, Luke mentions Anna, also a prophet (2:36–38).

All these references precede Pentecost which we have traditionally understood as the moment of the Holy Spirit. They remind us, therefore, that not only did Jesus send the Holy Spirit, but that in a certain sense the Holy Spirit sent Jesus (Crowe, 1989:324–343)—and Zechariah and Elizabeth, Mary and Simeon. The prophetic Spirit of God—sometimes called "Holy Spirit" without the definite article—is present throughout the history of salvation. One of the best-known references is in the prophecy of Joel, where God says:

I will pour out my spirit on all humankind. Your sons and daughters shall prophesy, your old men shall dream dreams, and your young ones see visions. Even on the slaves, men and women, will I pour out my spirit in those days....And all who call on Yahweh will be saved (Joel 2:28–29, 32).

This is four centuries before Jesus. It not only reminds the people of the presence of God's spirit in the community, but carries that tradition to a new level of development: God's spirit is not limited to people with official status, but is for "all humankind" as the text has it. *Each member* of the community is to be empowered.

If we take our tradition seriously, we will understand that participation in God's spirit implies *equal* status for each person in the community. How, then, might we apply the notion of prophecy to our lives as committed Christians? In theological terms, prophecy in its formal sense is the inspired delivery of God's message, not simply in word but also by action. Less formally, prophecy is a constant element of Christian witness, and we are all called to keep alive the hope of good news proclaimed by Jesus.

The Future of Care and Care of the Future

Someone—perhaps Karl Popper—said that the way a society cares for its most vulnerable and needy members is a measure of its own moral health. This simpleminded notion has profound implications. The most obviously vulnerable people are the very old and dependent, though infants and the unborn are just as needy. But the human community is not confined to the living; it includes the as-yet-unborn and the not-long-dead. The community of the living carries the responsibility for ensuring the group's continuation over many generations. Future members must be brought across life's threshold to birth; those who are dying must not be abandoned but carried across the threshold of death. But there are some not yet conceived, and others who have already died. Unless there is a respect for human life in principle, and specifically for the lives of others, a new generation may not be brought to birth or may be ill-prepared for life. Without respect for values embodied in the wise—specifically in the senior generation—the dead will be too quickly forgotten. And if their memory is erased, the stories of their lives will be lost and the community will be morally impoverished.

Today's rich nations seem to be suffering from a kind of cultural mania, a bipolar disorder which subjects people to wild swings between overconfidence and a great fear of death. Scientific experimentation and technological innovation are avidly encouraged. Human cloning is an ever-closer possibility. Attempts are made to throw a legal blanket over moral issues of life and death, living and dying, coming to birth and going to death. And yet many serious issues remain. Who will care for the vulnerable? Who will provide moral support? Where is the church? How is caring for people both an ecclesial commitment and a prophetic act? It is by no means easy to read the clouds during a time of rapid climatic change. But it is quite irresponsible for Christians to be swept along like tumbleweed.

The way we care for or neglect one another determines our destiny. One of the greatest moments of pathos in the whole gospel story is filled with the cry: "Lord, when was it that we saw you hungry or thirsty or a stranger or naked or sick or in prison, and did not take care of you?" (Mt 25:44). We cannot simply reflect on this intellectually; our whole way of being in the world with God—our spirituality—must be touched.

Our faith calls each of us to care for others. Yet such pastoral care must also be reflexive: *cura animarum* (care of others' souls) must be complemented by *cura sui* (the care of oneself). In the first generations of Christianity, before the religion became socially acceptable, believers developed the pastoral care of self as an essential precondition for the pastoral care of others. It "took the form of an attitude, a mode of behavior; it became instilled in ways of living; it evolved into procedures and formulas that people reflected on, perfected, and taught" (Foucault, 1986:45; Miles, 1990). We believe we are Temples of the Holy Spirit, and through our embodiment we share something essential with the Incarnate God. If disregard for others is sinful, then disregard for ourselves may be no less so.

Giuseppe di Lampedusa said, "If we want things to stay as they are, things will have to change." Whether or not we actually want them to change, things cannot stay the same. The future of organized pastoral care, particularly in the United States, seems to hang in the balance, for a variety of reasons. But some of the emerging questions are a direct challenge to our own lives as disciples. Is there really a widespread problem? Does it have anything to do with us? Will we adopt the "ostrich solution" and wait for the crisis to pass? Will we quietly carry on as before? But perhaps there is another approach. As Christians, are we not called, at an individual and local level first, to challenge social structures that discriminate against people? Must we not, by faith, show ourselves to be lovers, as committed to caring for the uncared-for as we are committed to caring for our own? Yet this challenge will not galvanize the fainthearted or those not supported by a strong community. Are there any hopeful avenues?

For about thirty years now, there has been a critical reappraisal of the contributions of the richer nations to the poorer. Words like *paternalism, imperialism,* and *proselytism* have been very painful to well-intentioned persons. Some people of faith, committed to ecclesial ministry of myriad kinds, are demoralized because their best pastoral efforts seem to be unappreciated. Others have made a crablike move in their ministerial commitments, only to end up feeling less like pastors or ministers and more like managers or bureaucrats.

There are dangerous cross-currents in pastoral care these days. Christians formally working as caregivers are among those most affected by sweeping changes in society. Jobs are being cut back, and even formal documents from Rome seem reactionary and discouraging. Certain elements within the medical establishment are not well-disposed to religious people who seek to bring comfort and care. And, as bureaucracy encroaches even further, some pastors and associates are tempted to become administrators at the expense of "hands-on" ministry to the sick or suffering.

If we Christians recognize that Western society's ambivalence about life and death, about sickness and therapy, borders on the pathological, we must make a stand. People committed to caring ministries must continue to be witnesses. We must offer a vigorous yet compassionate, counter-cultural and prophetic testimony to the importance of Jesus-like care—not merely for the sake of other believers but for the good of humanity.

"The most important thing is not survival but prophecy."

Thomas Merton's statement is itself prophetic, constituting a challenge to the rhetoric of those for whom "survival" and "progress" are clearly the greatest good. It is now past time for dissenting voices to be heard in the nation and for pathfinders to come forward and seek a way out of the desert and into the Promised Land, not of Utopia but of the Realm of God (Arbuckle, 1993). There is, in our day, a crying need for a spirituality for the long haul. We need a new model and vision of a healing community and a community of healers.

Here is a powerful example of pastoral caring from the Rivers State of Nigeria. It describes an annual ritual celebrated for many generations and perhaps even today.

On the appointed day, all the initiated adults of the community walk down to the river. Once assembled, they wade in the waist-high water and the drama begins. In a frenzy of shouting and screaming—mostly serious, some good-natured—insults and accusations are traded. People splash each other and sling mud from the river bed. Each person confronts anyone and everyone towards whom there is any anger or bitterness. The accumulated, pent-up hostility of the community is vented.

As the noise and splashing finally abate, each person, now covered in mud, ducks beneath the water and rinses off. Still submerged, they gather hands full of mud and debris, and rise in silence. On the river bank, a large cloth has been spread out. Everyone in turn dumps the contents of their hands on the cloth. The leader comes forward, takes the cloth by its corners, and ties it in a bundle. Nearby a goat is tethered, waiting, and the bundle is tied between its horns. The goat is now set loose and chased off into the undergrowth.

Silently the people return to the village. And from that day, nobody may raise a voice against another person in the group, or seek redress for anything that is now symbolically between the goat's horns. The past is past. The sins of the community have been car-

ried away. The community is now reconciled. Its wounds are healed. And each member of the community has been a witness to and a part of the healing.

Unhealthy Tradition

Most societies believe that their own approach to living is the best. Ancient Israel was afflicted by a superiority complex in relation to health, medicine, and the nature of community. If we can understand how *that* happened, we may be able to see better how the affluent nations today are touched by a similar complex. Perhaps, then, we can move toward attending to, ministering to, that particular affliction of the soul.

Israel created its cultural and religious identity by defining itself as opposed in principle to the surrounding cultures. It came to believe it had nothing whatsoever to learn from them. So it scorned what was actually the more advanced medical knowledge of these cultures. Israel knew little about the body and healing, and cared less. Its vocabulary of body-words was rudimentary: all of them referred to external, visible parts. Consistent with a self-important culture with a *Purity Code*, it came to treat sick or disabled people as unclean. Occasionally, they were seen as made imperfect by God in order to be the future object of Divine intervention (Stuhlmueller, 1989). But illness itself, and thus sick people, gradually became marginalized, exploited, or abandoned. In time, this attitude became socially and religiously accepted, canonized through the codification of the theology that had created it in the first place.

Unconcerned with the body and ignorant of anything beyond gross anatomy and physiology, the culture of ancient Israel boasted few diagnostic skills and focused largely on externals. God was understood as a powerful God of the living or of life, identified with *health* or *perfection* (cf: Deut 5:26; 1 Sam 17:26; Is

37:4). Its theology of healthcare was thus underdeveloped almost to the point of nonexistence.

The surrounding peoples—Egyptians, Canaanites, Philistines—were different. They did not separate the care of the sick from their religious practice. In fact the two were directly related. Cultural practices like surgery and mummification provided the Egyptians with a very sophisticated understanding of the human body and its processes, and in consequence produced a rich vocabulary. The Hebrew language, however, did not even have specific words for lungs, stomach, or nervous system. Pagan temples, generally, including sanctuaries or spas, were frequently places for the sick. Actually, before the Exile, Israel was relatively tolerant of such places. Later though, due perhaps to a combined siege-mentality and sense of self-importance, it became strongly opposed to them. In the whole Mosaic Law, the Pentateuch, there is not an unequivocal good word about health care!

Israel repudiated all the wisdom particular to other cultures, including their understanding of God's (or the gods') concern about the weak and needy, the sick and disabled. This, of course, bred ignorance. And ignorance combined with the absence of legal regulations governing health, provided a breeding ground for quacks and honey-tongued charlatans operating in the shadows. Because of Israel's cultural and religious isolationism and superiority complex, accompanied by *Purity Code* and priestly caste, sickness was perceived simply to create impurity and contamination and to be a sign of Divine disfavor. The status of attendants (ministers) and physicians was therefore low, and such people were largely regarded as illegitimate recourse. The sick had little choice but to seek help clandestinely, at pagan shrines. But the price of any healing would be a guilty conscience, if not shunning by the community.

King Asa is used as an object lesson by the contemptuous writer of Second Chronicles. Here are three versions of the passage, (2 Chr 6:12):

The *Jerusalem Bible* says:
a disease attacked Asa from head to foot…and what is more he turned in his sickness not to Yahweh, but to doctors.

The *Good News Bible* is more scathing:
Asa was crippled by a severe foot disease; but even then he did not turn to Yahweh but to doctors.

And here is the *New RSV:*
Asa was diseased in his feet, and his disease became severe; yet even in his disease he did not seek the LORD, *but sought help from physicians.*

The Prophetic Alternative

Before the Exile in the sixth century B.C.E., the Temple was still a more or less legitimate place for people to seek solace for their ills. As fears of religious impurity and cultural contamination created exclusiveness, the Priestly Code "severely restricted access to the Temple for the chronically ill"; moreover it "minimizes state responsibility for the ill, leaving the eradication of illness for the future" (Metzger and Coogan, 1993:508). As a result, people suffering from a wide range of illnesses were now excluded from the community. This had two consequences. There was now an embarrassment of chronically sick populations with no access to the Temple. But perhaps worse, there was now a formal theological justification for this appalling state of affairs.

Yet the counter-cultural or prophetic element is never completely muted. God is never left entirely without witnesses. People are called to a more godly perception; and, even though prophets are often harshly treated, there is always some indication, however grudging, that God is indeed greater than human descriptions or theological formulas. Jeremiah's voice is boldly raised, "a rebel against the restrictions of the Jerusalem priesthood" (Stuhlmueller, 1989:6). And who can forget Isaiah 58? This is Post-Exilic, part of a great hymn about the hope of restoration. It echoes the litany in Matthew's Gospel, describing the Last Judgment. It is a call to justice, and to prophetic commitment. Here are a few verses, edited and with emphasis added:

Is not this the fast that I choose: to loose the bonds of injustice, to share your bread with the hungry, and bring the homeless poor into your house; and not to hide yourself from your own kin? Then your light shall break forth like the dawn, and your healing shall spring up quickly. Then you shall call, and the LORD *will answer; you shall cry for help, and he will say, Here I am. If you remove the yoke, the pointing of the finger, the speaking of evil, if you offer your food to the hungry and satisfy the needs of the afflicted, then your light shall rise in the darkness. The* LORD *will guide you continually, and satisfy your needs, and make your bones strong; and you shall be like a watered garden. You shall be called the restorer of streets to live in* (Isa 58:6–12).

The book of Ecclesiasticus, from the second century B.C.E., maintains the prophetic thrust of justice. The author, Ben Sirach, was widely traveled and open to the wisdom of other nations (Sir 39:2–4). Perhaps this is why, in spite of very conservative theology and some extremely limited (and perhaps offensive) comments, he can still see God's hand in healing and healers, and God's presence in the sick and afflicted. He is quite clear that the sacrifices of those who oppress the poor are *not* acceptable to God (Sir 35:14–15). Fearlessly, he declaims the serious civic obligation to practice social justice and assist the weak and defenseless (Sir 3:30–31; 4:2–6,8–10) (Metzger and Coogan, 1993:697–699). This is the epitome of the kind of pastoral care the every Christian, in some measure, is called to minister:

Honor physicians for their services, for the Lord created them; their gift of healing comes from the Most High. The skill of physicians makes them distinguished. The Lord created medicines out of the earth, and the sensible will not despise them. [God] gave skill to human beings. By them the physician heals and takes away pain; the pharmacist makes a mixture from them (38:1–7).

Again:

Give up your faults, and direct your hands rightly, and cleanse your heart from all sin. Offer a sweet-smelling sacrifice and a memorial portion. Then give the physician his place, for the Lord created him; do not let him leave you, for you need him. There may come a time when recovery lies in the hands of physicians, for they too pray to the Lord that [God] grant them success in diagnosis, and in healing, for the sake of preserving life (Sir 38:10–14).

Not only is this a tremendously strong endorsement of medical skills and ministry, it is a wonderful exaltation of what we might call *integrated pastoral care*. Regrettably, the writer does fall back on the much more traditional understanding, saying "My son, when you are ill do not be depressed, but pray to the Lord and he will heal you." There would be nothing wrong with this if it did not effectively make prayer the *only* recommended and worthy course of action, relying totally on God's direct intervention and not even partly on the knowledge or skills of the physician. Still, he did rise to the occasion and voice a rather counter-cultural and prophetic vision.

There are also further faint but unmistakable traces of a prophetic response to outcasts: those people designated as such by their culture or religion. Brave souls these prophets, many of them anonymous; they actually went in search of the outcast. They declared that negative, judgmental, and prejudiced human understanding was *not* an authentic, godly perspective. The books of Amos, Isaiah, Joshua, Judges, Samuel, and 1 and 2 Kings all contain examples of such prophetic insight and speech. The story of Elijah and the dead son of the widow of Zarephath is a good illustration. In reaching out and touching the corpse, Elijah deliberately rendered himself unclean by the religious standards of his time (1 Kg 17:17). But prophecy is always willing to break through and speak out, though often it is the tiniest and least audible of voices.

The truly prophetic voice never allowed people to be separated from other people or from the wider community. Nor did it drive a wedge between body and soul, nor physical healing from spiritual well-being. The authentic tradition *integrated* bodily and emotional and spiritual healing. In other words, it was committed to the well-being of *soul:* a truth attested by the fact that the Hebrew verb *rapha* (heal) is always joined with *shub* (return home/convert) (Hos 11:1–4; 14:1–2). Ironically, the people often misunderstood God in these matters, and Hosea has God saying that the people have not understood that God was in fact the one looking after them: "They did not know that I healed them" (Hos 11:3).

The prophetic tradition would always attest to the fact that the unclean, especially the sick, crippled, and the otherwise disabled, would be the *first* to be part of the new kingdom. Here is probably the very latest part of Isaiah, composed around 300 B.C.E. Israel needed to hear such a voice as this, but so do we:

Be strong, do not fear! Here is your God. God will come and save you. Then the eyes of the blind shall be opened, and the ears of the deaf unstopped; then the lame shall leap like a deer, and the tongue of the speechless sing for joy. Everlasting joy shall be upon their heads; they shall obtain joy and gladness, and sorrow and sighing shall flee away (Isa 35:5,6,10).

Jesus and Prophetic Care

John the Baptist's followers approached Jesus because they wanted to know if he was the one who was expected. After centuries since the first prophecies of Isaiah, this has already been a long wait. In words that echo Isaiah, Jesus says:

Go and tell John what you have seen and heard: the blind receive their sight, the lame walk, the lepers are cleansed, the deaf hear, the dead are raised, the poor have good news brought to them. And blessed is anyone who takes no offense at me (Lk 7:22–23).

Here is *restoration* (the blind *receive* or *regain* their sight). Here is fulfillment of age-old expectation. Here is the prophetic action of one who refused to make distinctions between people. And this is the measure of commitment for anyone who aspires to extending God's reign. It is, of course, what we might call the *Jesus Program.* If we want to be caring persons in the spirit of Jesus, it is the challenge before us.

Not only would Jesus speak words of healing and lay healing hands on the needy, he would make it his life's work. Everything Jesus does is healing in some sense. Every journey he makes becomes an encounter with people on the margins, at the edges, under the crushing burdens. Far from simply "ministering" to them and then carrying on with his own life, his own life is actually *defined* by his ministry to them. This fuses his world and theirs, and makes him one with them: an outcast, a pariah, or in one of Crossan's fine phrases, a nobody creating a kingdom of nobodies.

In Jesus' ministry, every healing story has a double thread. The narrative line shows how a person or a group receives healing; but, often submerged, there is a more subtle challenge. The wider community is called to learn a deeper lesson and apply it to its fundamental belief system and its very understanding of God. Jesus the prophet will disclose forgotten or unknown aspects of God. He will speak of God's compassion for every single person, and God's utter lack of vindictiveness or partiality. He will preach good news of community and inclusion and hope to a people steeped in a world of hierarchy and exclusion and fatalistic despair. This will bring upon him the opprobrium and self-righteousness of the privileged classes. It will also have such liberating potential for despised and condemned people as to give them a new lease on life, turning at least some of them into a community of radical itinerants or healed healers.

If the human spirit lacks nurture and challenge it begins to suffer from spiritual decline. This is seen in a depletion or slowing down: not just slowness but *sloth*. It is marked by flagging zeal, which is very life-threatening to Christian ministers. Thus it is crucial for successive generations to rediscover the power of prophetic discipleship.

Our generation of Christians stands on the edge: the dangerous edge. We face a crisis of human values and community care. Will we move courageously forward in imitation of Jesus the compassionate and risk-taking lover and healer? Or will our faint-heartedness and conservatism, our tiredness and lack of faith, win out and turn us back from the challenge facing us and the future of pastoral care? Perhaps the pastoral strategy and tactics of Jesus will give us heart.

Healing Faith

Jesus goes in search of one thing: faith. Not a full-blown, formal creed, but a spark of trust that there is more to life than suffering and incapacity, that there is indeed someone who cares. Jesus, the suffering servant, is the one who will not extinguish that spark, that "smoldering wick" (Isa 42:3), but will fan it into flame. Faith, then, is all he wants, and a tinge of hope that God will continue to be God in spite of what some theologians and some theology may say. But Jesus does not want to "play God" either in a theatrical or in a self-important way. He wants only to be the vehicle of God's healing care. As such, he tries to persuade other people that their own faith can make a radical difference.

Ironically, of course, Jesus tends to find faith where it is least expected or most dramatic. And he sometimes searches vainly among the very people who might be expected to be faith-filled. As the Cameroonian theologian Eboussi Boulaga said: "Miracles do not make faith: faith makes miracles." Samaritans, Syrophoenicians, Roman centurions, widows, women in prostitution, men in dubious occupations, and people with mental sickness—as well as a whole range of others, classed as outcasts or sinners by virtue of social position or physical sickness—these are the people from whom faith, tinged with hope, comes pouring. And healing follows, as well as Jesus' sometimes astonished praisesong: "Truly I tell you, in no one in Israel have I found such faith" (Mt 8:10).

However, where there is no faith, Jesus can do little or nothing. Sometimes, it is the *lack* of faith that astonishes him! (Mk 6:1–6). He remonstrates with his hapless disciples, calling them names: "You faithless generation. How much longer must I be among you? How much longer must I put up with you?" (Mk 9:19). And when they look for an explanation for their failure to be part of a healing community, Jesus says bluntly that some people's demons can only be dispelled (and some people only be brought to healing) by faithful prayer (Mk 9:29).

It is not only the lack of faith, the laziness, that Jesus finds objectionable in some of the leaders and in his disciples: their theology itself is diseased and needs to be purified. This can be seen very well in the story of the man born blind (Jn 9): healing blindness and other physical incapacities is often considerably easier than healing people's assumptions. So the questions once again challenge us: can we read the clouds that gather over our own confused generation? And what can we deduce and apply, as we commit to care in the future?

First, we are called to various forms of ministry *primarily* through our baptism. And second, Jesus constantly reminds us of the strength of community. Wherever Jesus is, nobody is excluded and absolutely everyone is invited to be involved in the healing ministry.

The intentions of Jesus concerning healing and restoration cannot possibly be confined to his own time or place, or to his own encounters. Nor are Peter, or James or John, the Twelve or the Seventy-Two, the only people significant enough to be healers. The entire ministry of Jesus is marked by healing, and Jesus promises that believers will do the same and even more (Jn 14:12), and that where there are two or three he is with them (Mt 18:20). What is needed, and apparently is sufficient, is a combination of personal faith and healing community: "Jesus implies that while an external acceptance by the community is necessary for the minister to heal, so is a spiritual sensitivity and dependence on God by the minister. Healing requires both an external and an internal spiritual environment" (Rosenblatt, 1989:15). Unless our communities and parishes and dioceses and churches are encouraged and prodded to take increasing responsibility for supporting integrated care of human beings—pastoral care—we will fail as a Christian people.

If it was possible in the past, it is surely not possible today for us to bracket the missionary and prophetic element of our Christian calling and to leave those things to others. We have a responsibility to ensure that our spirituality is missionary and prophetic: a tall order indeed! We know that all truly missionary ministry is centrifugal. It reaches out and includes in. We know that all truly prophetic ministry speaks out and speaks up. Both are concerned with integrity and truth: God's. Each demands a commitment on our part to discern God working in the world and in people. Left to ourselves we become narrow, prejudiced, comfortable, and lazy. But we cannot be part-time Christians. Christianity itself demands a radical commitment.

Without entertaining illusions of grandeur, we simply may not shirk the prophetic dimension of our calling. To do so would be at best to fall for "Band-Aid-ism": at worst, a kind of apostasy. We may have to speak out and speak up, for there is much brokenness and many suffering people.

To be prophetic in the face of pastoral need is not simply a matter of being outspoken. Political action is only part of what is needed. To be prophetic is to commit to risk and hope, like Jesus. To be a prophetic people is to be a people of faith, a moral community, a communion of saints. But faith is not naive or credulous belief in miracles, much less is it waiting passively for something to happen. Rather, it is to believe fervently and intensely, to hope against hope, to bring about or "midwife" the miracle that will surely come because it is promised to faithful, faith-filled people. The age of miracles will last as long as the age of believers and prophets endures. But the miracles which come through faith will be something entirely unforeseeable, neither a stay of execution nor a clumsy extension of the old order. We have no idea of what is yet to come, but to imagine that our best is behind us—institutionally or inspirationally—is to have already lost hope. The *terminus ad quem*, the point toward which things are tending, is something quite new: it will not be discovered by drawing a line from the past to the present and then extending it into the future. That may be a rational procedure but it is not God's way, for God's Spirit will make all things *new*.

All of this is not only meant to be encouraging, but represents yet another invitation for us: as the prophet says, God will show portents in the heavens (Joel 2:30). Jesus was saddened, angry, frustrated, even bewildered by people's refusal, reluctance, or inability to read the clouds. Prophets are needed, people who will venture out and look at us and cross boundaries and engage the unknown. They challenge the *status quo* and flourish where there are lies and half-truths. Our times must call them forth so that people may hear their voice.

Early Christian practice, exemplified in the Epistle of James, was to refuse to accept illness as Divine punishment or as impossible to address. But in our day this abomination is creeping back into our consciousness. Susan Sontag (1989) showed how illnesses have been widely identified with evil, but more significantly with God's vindictiveness. She demonstrates how in these days AIDS is now replacing TB, cancer, syphilis, and other "demonic" or "retributive" diseases in the public mind. We are surely aware of Christians who claim that such diseases are the direct action of a vindictive God. But this was precisely what Jesus' healing was intended to counteract. God does not use sickness either as threat or as weapon. And today's carers, taking the missionary and prophetic dimensions of their baptism with particular urgency, must continue this healing and restorative message. It is challenging and may sometimes be counter-cultural, but it is of God. Prophecy must be willing to break barriers and tend to the living sick (Stuhlmueller, 1989), as we see when Peter took the lame man by the hand and healed him in the name of Jesus Christ (Acts 3:2–7).

Can We Measure Up?

What kind of Christians are we? What kind of caregivers do we aspire to be? It is so easy to lose the common touch and become distanced from the community, the People of God, those who suffer. Perhaps a few warnings may be appropriate.

First, we can easily fall prey to an exclusivist or elitist mentality, especially in relation to the realities of the poor or outcasts in our society, the prisoners or those suffering from what we used to call "social diseases." We may find ourselves comfortable at the centers, forgetting that the prophetic edge is keenest at some distance from the center, and does not fear being somewhat eccentric. Prophets are, after all, to be found, not inside the temple, but outside it or in front if it. *Pro fanum,* "profane," means to be "in front of the temple": to be separated from the holy and righteous inside!

At the center of every fruit we find the core and the pit: closer to the edge is where the flesh is, and the flavor and the savor. Jesus favored the places and the people who lived some way from the center!

Second, there seems to be an insufficiently-examined assumption that religious life today is on the "cutting edge." This would imply that public institutions like congregations and orders exist as prophetic signs in society. If recent scandals in religious institutions have not persuaded us of the partial untruth of this, perhaps another consideration will. Institutions *as such* are inherently conservative. Individuals or small groups are much more likely to be on the edge, "cutting" or otherwise. And individuals or small groups who follow Jesus are faithful and radical disciples first, and only incidentally members of institutions.

Again, we may actually believe that certain kinds of sickness are punishment. But that would make our God both vindictive and exclusivist. Then, instead of learning from sickness and the human condition, we may simply repeat Old Testament igno-rance and disreputable priestly-code attitudes.

Fourth, it is easy, especially in a climate of competitiveness and job insecurity, for ministry of care to become a "service in-dustry" dispensing sacrament-and-fortune-cookie moralizing. If so, what has the Incarnation meant? What is the significance of Jesus, "like us in all things but sin"? Jesus took us far beyond our narrow horizons (Nolan, 1992). Have we regressed? Have our notions of caring for one another as a fruit of our faith been forgotten in the face of dominant culture values and slogans like "managed care"? If so, we must seek new ways of being a Chris-tian community, a prophetic Christian community, for we are called to speak. Christians have done so before, and urgently need to do so again.

Here is part of a mid second-century letter describing the Christian community:

In a word, what the soul is in the body, that the Christians are in the world. The soul is spread through all the members of the body, and the Christians throughout the cities of the world. The soul dwells in the body, but is not part and parcel of the body; so Christians dwell in the world but are not of the world. Christians are known as such in the world, but their religion remains invisible. The world, though suffering no wrong from Christians, hates them because they oppose its pleasures. Christians love those that hate them. Chris-tians are shut up in the world as in a prison, but themselves sustain the world. Christians, when penalized, show a daily increase in numbers on that account. God has appointed them to so great a post, and they are not at liberty to desert it (Quasten, 1948).

We do not speak our own words, but we proclaim what Jesus proclaimed: the good news of healing restoration. Much special interest surrounds medicine and healthcare these days. There is need for plain speaking and courageous witness to the fact that sickness and death must be faced squarely. Not by running from or denying their existence do people and society come to wholeness. Only by being truthful and supportive do we show true concern for the weak, the exposed, the unproductive, and the unlovely. Whether there are enough paid jobs or funds for everyone, pastoral care will always be a Christian imperative.

Finally, no streamlining of social and healthcare services will compensate for the rediscovery of soul and of prayer. Some of us may have to learn (more exactly perhaps, to be taught), to pray with our families or communities, especially in times of sickness. A little prayer together can be the most effective communication, both with each other and with God. We are called and sent to speak reconciliation and restoration, healing and hope. Anyone who is more afraid of a sick human being or a corpse than of being disloyal to the "dangerous memory" of Jesus is not yet a disciple.

If we are tainted by what is not of God in dominant culture attitudes, we will feel the need personally to make everything turn out "OK." But Jesus invites us to pray to God in a different way: *fiat voluntas tua:* "may *your* will be done"; and "give us this day our daily bread" [our daily requirements]. Or as Peter said so poignantly: "Lord, to whom shall we go? You have the words of everlasting life."

We claim no personal power over the words of everlasting life, but we are called to be filled with the Spirit and the Word. It is our responsibility as Christians—pastors, associates, caregivers of all kinds—to commit ourselves prophetically to this apostolate, lest the mighty wind we whip up be not the Spirit of God but merely our own hot air, and lest our well-wrought phrases be not the words of God's healing promise but only our own, hollowly-echoing words.

Chapter Six

Embodied Spirituality

Through joy the beauty of the world penetrates our soul. Through suffering it penetrates our body.

SIMONE WEIL

The soul needs vernacular life—relationship to a local place and culture. The soul needs an intense, full-bodied spiritual life as much as and in the same way that the body needs food.

THOMAS MOORE

The worth of a religious life depends ultimately not on what can be conceived but on what can be embodied.

MARGARET MILES

Taking the Incarnation Literally

The first chapter of Genesis tells the Creation story. At every stage God paused and saw that it was good. Seven times. The final occasion marks the creation of humanity. Made in God's own image, male and female, Adam and Eve receive a special blessing (Gen 1:28). There is great promise and great hope, followed by great disappointment, for God's own people did not accept their place in the world.

John's Gospel continues the story: Jesus, the Christ, truly God, becomes a member of the human community. From the beginning the Creator forged an intimate relationship with people; now the Spirit breathes new life into that relationship in a most remarkable way. Man and woman were created in God's image and likeness; now God is enfleshed in the image and likeness of humanity. Again there is great promise and great hope; again it is followed by great disappointment, for "his own people did not accept him" (Jn 1:11).

This story contains a profound lesson. We are not God, yet God invites us to come very close; and God is not us, though God is very "down to earth" (Phil 2:6–8). The task of humanity, redeemed in Jesus, is to remember both parts of the lesson. But we forget. Some of us forget we are not God: arrogant pride is a besetting danger for ambitious people. Others forget we are indeed human, of the earth: neglect of our bodies, of our *embodied selves*, is no less hazardous. It is not only sad but tragic that we Christians have had such an inconsistent relationship with our bodies; rarely have we been content to be as God made us. This is quite insulting to God. But there is more: Jesus became as we are—human, embodied, *incarnate*—but we fail to take him seriously. The consequences have been dreadful. Over centuries we have underestimated the humanity of Jesus and failed to live in a godly manner in, through, and with our bodies. And when one thinks of how Christians—often in the name of God—have treated other human beings, likewise made in God's image, we should be ashamed.

We say we believe we are made in God's image. We say we believe that Jesus took flesh and became a human person, born of Mary, like us in all things but sin. We claim to believe that Jesus, the Christ, truly God, became truly human. Yet throughout history we have rarely been as willing to embrace the humanness of Jesus as to worship his divinity. Apart from keeping us from recognizing Jesus as one of us, it has meant in a very profound sense that we have failed to recognize ourselves! If we are made in God's image, we have a spark of divinity; if God is made human in the Incarnation, then God has a spark of humanity.

For a thousand years, Christians perceived Jesus overwhelmingly in his divinity, and the Church had great struggles with doctrinal excesses such as Docetism and Monophysitism: Jesus was from above, and thus most completely *un*like the rest of humanity. If he was "in the form of God," it was almost as if God were playing games or dressing up. True God he was: but hardly true man. So the immense honor God bestowed on us by becoming *truly* human—incarnate, embodied, one like us—often went virtually unnoticed. Since Descartes in the seventeenth century, body has been even more subordinated to mind: "I think therefore I am." Body-as-machine is purely functional, making no significant contribution to our fundamental identity. And dualistic thinking continues to stalk us. But how can we identify with a Jesus who only pretends to be embodied as human? We do not *have* bodies as we have shoes. We are inseparable from our bodies: that is how we exist. When our bodies cease to live they become corpses: our very *selves* cease to live. We cannot live only as soul or spirit, because we are human—enfleshed, embodied, incarnated.

Questions arise. If everyone is made in God's image, what is the importance of human differences as a reflection of who God is? If Jesus became as we are, what more do we need to know about who "we" are, in a world of six billion embodied persons (for surely the "we" is not simply "people like me")? How does each of us accept, engage, use, and offer our embodied lives back to God in appropriate worship?

Reading the clouds is our responsibility. But there are many kinds of clouds, and they bear many messages. Until we notice particular cloud formations we cannot begin to interpret them. So it is with people. Committed to the inclusive and boundary-breaking mission of Jesus, we are called—each of us in some fashion—to go beyond familiar people and places. Jesus says that whatever we do to other people we do to him. How will we relate to Jesus as he is discovered in many different people? Even his own did not recognize him (Jn 1:10–11). How might we fail to recognize and welcome Jesus, because we are not receptive to people different from ourselves?

Understanding Through Our Bodies

"Therefore a man leaves his father and his mother and clings to his wife, and they become one flesh" (Gen 2:24). Leaving and cleaving are basic human activities. When emphasis is placed on one, the other is affected. The Creation story explicitly identifies human unity and integration with physical bonding and em-bodiment—rather than with the ability to speak, or to make contracts, or other aspects of humanness: how we behave is more important than what we say.

Language employs words and ideas that are capable of separating and distinguishing. Bodiliness is expressed by human persons capable of embracing and bonding. Bodiliness is more powerful than any single language: it is the basis for universal understanding. Bodiliness can say the unsayable. This is what happens in human rituals, which create community (Jackson, 1983:341). It is also accomplished by human love.

Perhaps that is one of the reasons Jesus seeks out the politically powerless and socially marginal. They are grounded, even constrained, by their physicality and this-worldliness, which may make them realistic and down to earth in a way that would connect them with the redeemer and restorer of humanity. The poor live in their bodies more than anyone else does. They have no refrigerators or air-conditioners, no snacks and cocktails, no thermal coats or insulated homes to protect them from reality. They may be more accessible to the God who goes in search of those who have strayed.

All theological language is analogical and self-committing. If we image God as totally other and self-sufficient, we demean the idea of a real covenant—with its associations of mutual exchange and relationship—and we effectively cut ourselves off from God. But the unbridgeable divide between God and ourselves has already been bridged by Jesus. Why, in our desire to maintain God's absoluteness, have we found it so difficult to embrace the humanity of Jesus or to live as if we truly believed that God is with us? Jesus' whole life is marked by his encounters, embraces, touches—his embodied self. He presents himself as a man who experiences hunger and thirst, the need to sleep, to bathe, to congregate, to celebrate, to reach out. His ministry would have been impossible if he had not been so available, so identifiably human. His humanness was palpable: people could literally reach him, touch him, feed him, speak with him, beat him, and crucify him. We may need to reflect on this.

Jesus' embodiment was no pretense: it was essential to his identity. Embodiment is also essential to our own identity. We are moral persons in and through our bodies. The test of our acceptability as followers of Jesus is that we do what he did: feed the hungry, give drink to the thirsty, clothe the naked, welcome the stranger.

Our language or religion or dress or customs may make us unintelligible and inaccessible to people of different religions and cultures or conventions. But in our embodiment we are accessible, able to be identified and encountered precisely as human. Unless, as we encounter one another, we are aware of our em-

bodiment—somewhat self-conscious in fact—we will fail to encounter one another authentically. This is because all our experience is body-mediated. Our bodies link us in a network as broad
as our imagination, for it is "the power of mutual imaginability"
that makes for human unity (Hastrup, 1993:733). Consequently,
the more we encounter others and recognize in their faces a reflection of our own and even of God's, the more we will be seeing things from God's perspective. And until we can identify God
in everyone, we will have a very limited and ethnocentric understanding of God. This, of course, is what faith is about.

If we have failed to live and encounter and worship in and
through our bodies, then we have also failed to acknowledge
human imperfection. Our bodies are not perfect: as human persons we are imperfect and incomplete; and God wishes to restore us. But God also wishes to encourage us—as Jesus taught—
to lay hands on one another and make community, and to restore one another! If we were physically perfect we might attempt
to survive without other people. Not being so, we might actually
find community and support, if we are prepared to acknowledge
our human reality.

Embodying a Jesus Attitude

Jesus said, "Follow me and I will make you fish for *people*" (Mt
4:19): not *souls*, or spirits, but human persons. Perhaps we might
do a thought experiment, and follow Jesus through the towns
and villages, eavesdrop at tables and in houses, and try to identify his own pastoral strategy.

Quite simply, Jesus starts off by loving. His approach is to encounter, reach out, embrace, forgive, heal, include. He searches
for faith, but also inspires and kindles it. And all this by the sheer
attractiveness of his noncondemnatory, healing approach.

Not that he compromises on truth or values, but never does

he lose sight of the dignity of the person. Never does he demean or treat people without respect. Never does he manipulate or subordinate them to some grand plan. He meets them in their particular human condition, in their suffering, wounded, hungry, depleted bodies. Since people feel and recognize their human need primarily in terms of their physical needs, not surprisingly Jesus is attracted to and attracts those with some bodily needs. Pastoral difficulties arise only when he encounters people who claim to be self-sufficient, and thereby become self-righteous, hypocritical, insensitive or unjust toward others. Before all else, his outreach is intended to heal and to restore.

Loving, healing, restoring: words describing the behavior and actions of a flesh-and-blood person; they fit Jesus. Judging, correcting, changing: the vocabulary of the mind; it fits…ourselves? Why is such language so frequently associated (particularly by people who are not Christian) with people who purport to act in Jesus' name? Unless we identify such aspects in ourselves, and turn and be converted, we will fail to do what Jesus did and what Jesus calls us to do in his name.

Human beings are culturally and religiously judgmental. We have strong ideas not only about what is right, true, and good, but about what is wrong, false, and bad. Those of us with years of formal education learn to analyze and judge, and are rewarded for doing so. Consequently we approach situations intellectually. Our brain is often the first part of ourselves to become engaged, and this is probably more true of men than of women. Yet men have claimed preeminence in continuing the work of Jesus!

But the way of Jesus is different. His pastoral plan does not unfold from a mental blueprint but from actual encounters with real persons. He touches and embraces, becomes a friend and companion, eats and drinks with a wide variety of people. He engages with individuals and with crowds, and is at ease with strangers and people of many different backgrounds. Women and other socially marginalized people are particularly attracted to him. His patience and availability are quite astounding and often irksome to his male disciples. They wanted Jesus to get rid of the crowds (Mt 14:15–16), but Jesus fed five thousand; they scolded Bartimaeus, but Jesus restored his sight (Mk 10:48). And throughout his public life he is committed to reconciling and healing and loving. Jesus models an integrated life of action and prayer, outreach and contemplation. His personal warmth is frequently attested not simply by the flocking crowds but by his encounters with individuals. In Jesus we encounter God Incarnate.

What of Christ's followers over the centuries? In our thought experiment we might consider Christians we have known. Generally speaking, are they convincingly human, glad to be alive, engagingly physical, warmly personable, and loving? Do they impress by their outreach and inclusiveness, their embraces and their touch, their engagement and availability, their trust and mutuality? Do they glory in being fully alive, fully human? Do they seek to follow Jesus—the human, itinerant, pastoral, risk-taking Jesus? Or do they project a certain lack of ease with their bodies, a certain denial of the physical, an unattractive asceticism and overemphasis on the intellectual? Does their body language speak tension between openness and self-control, trust and self-discipline, bodiliness and spirituality, this-worldliness and other-worldliness, feeling and thinking? And how do we imagine other people see us?

If, historically and theologically, Christians have yearned to be out of the body or acted as if they despised or were embarrassed by it, what does this say about respect for God's providential plan for human beings in general and for Jesus in particular? The Word was made flesh and dwelt among us. This is Incarnation! God who became human flesh and blood in Jesus was communication and gift. In the body of Christ, God spoke and touched and embraced and healed. The humanness of Jesus, specifically his embodiment, was the very instrument of evangelization. Historically, God did not only speak from a cloud on a mountaintop, but from the mouth of Jesus of Nazareth; historically, God assured the people, not only through pillars of fire or manna in the desert, but through the healing words of Jesus. This is what the Incarnation means: we can better grasp the idea of God because of Jesus.

Long before there was church and seven sacraments, Jesus invited everyone to come and find reconciliation, compassion, and hope. Our job as Christians, the Body of Christ, is to continue to embody the same reconciliation and compassion and hope. If we fail, it is not because we are not God, but because we are not yet the Body of Christ.

A Healing Touch

Healing is to the body as teaching is to the mind. People who are ill at ease with the body, who subordinate it or minimize its importance, will be unlikely to commit themselves to healing as authentic ministry. Those who enthrone the mind will tend to adopt an intellectual or rational approach to ministry. Each emphasis can find support in a partial reading of the instructions of Jesus.

But no partial reading does justice to his ministry and memory. True, he proclaimed a message, but it was certainly not limited to a verbal proclamation. His words were often *performative*: he *did* what he *said* he was doing. He actually forgave, healed, restored people. Healing was at the heart of Jesus' ministry. And he gave the same authority "to cure every disease and every sickness" (Mt 10:1; cf Mk 16:17), as well as to judge and forgive (Jn 20:23). But this was a gift not only for the closest disciples but for *every single believer* in his own ministry: "Very truly, I tell you, the one who believes in me will also do the works that I do and, in fact, will do greater works than these" (Jn 14:12).

What has happened? In fact, if not in theory, the church's healing ministry has been subordinated to the teaching ministry. Certain unhealthy forms of hierarchy have usurped the place of the mutuality and equality that Jesus strove to establish. And in what is probably not just a coincidence but direct result, body has been subordinated to mind and women to men. But in Jesus there is supposed to be no subordination—of healing, of body, or of woman. Differences, of course, exist, and varieties of gifts, services, and activities; "but it is the same God *who activates all of them in everyone*" (1 Cor 12:4–6). Furthermore, differences are never raised to the level of moral distinctions or hierarchy: there will always be men and women, just as there will always be Jews and Greeks, and even slaves and free persons, but *in Christ all are one* (Gal 3:28). Yet classically in Christian history, teaching has been the most privileged expression of ministry, and men—the teachers—have been the central figures. Thus healing has occupied a subordinate position, and women—the people most involved in healing ministry—have been marginalized. It is a tragedy that should never have happened. Disintegration is now a life-threatening disease in the rich and privileged nations:

Our world is on the verge of self-destruction and death because the society as a whole has so deeply neglected that which is most human and most valuable, and the most basic of all the works of love— the work of human communication, of caring and nurturance, of tending the personal bonds of community. This activity has been seen as women's work, and discounted as too mundane and undramatic, too distracting from the serious business of world-rule (Harrison, 1981:47).

In trying to identify the divine plan, the official Church is careful to describe men's and women's ministerial contributions as distinct but diverse, rather than as inferior and superior. The *magisterium* also struggles to interpret the significance, not only of the humanity of Jesus, but specifically his maleness. Nevertheless we are far from perfect. If any of us (Christians, the church) have identified men as hierarchically superior to women, males as intrinsically preferred to females, teaching as superior and therefore men's work, and healing as inferior and therefore women's, then we have perpetrated a sacrilege: we have put asunder what God, in Jesus, joined together.

If Jesus' work was healing as much as it was teaching, then what has been designated women's work is equally Jesus' "good-news-ing" work. But it is time to move beyond competitiveness in these matters; that happens when differences are not seen as complementary or as equally significant. Competition is not a mark or sign of the Christian community. In his ministry, Jesus moved toward integration and restoration. If Christ's body is still marked by division and competition and muted anathemas, then far from healing and reconciling in his name we are continuing to crucify him in his members.

A measure of discipleship and faithful commitment to Jesus is found when the Son of Man comes to judge (Mt 25:31ff). Favorable judgment, consisting of a blessing and an invitation into the kingdom, depends upon what we used to call the corporal works of mercy. Far from being something we do to bodies alone (there is no mention of preparing corpses or burying the dead), they are works of the living, designed to heal and restore, to maintain and enhance humanness. As embodied persons we serve one another through our bodies. Therefore we are to feed, clothe, welcome, nurture, and visit (the "corporal" works). Not only is this a measure of our respect for other human persons; above all it is a measure of our response to God. Little wonder that, according to the gospel, both the righteous and the accursed will be surprised that God is presented as embodied. The miracle is that some, the righteous, respond to the existential needs of others. That is a measure of their response to God, and of God's requirements of them. "Just as you did it to one of the least of these who are members of my family, you did it to me" (Mt 25:40).

Cross-Cultural Contact

If we feel sorry for those who fail to recognize God in the poor and needy, at least we can try to learn the lesson they failed to learn. God is presented as actually embodied in the myriad persons who populate the world. What are the pastoral implications? First, we understand God in Jesus to be God-with-us, God body-and-soul, God human-and-divine. Therefore we must believe that God is morally involved and invested with all of creation, including all of humanity. So "nothing happens to the world that does not also happen to God" (McFague, 1993:176). This is not pantheism, and it resonates strongly with the message of the Last Judgment. God is not reduced to the world, but McFague does say that God suffers and rejoices with those who suffer and rejoice. If we are to be with God, then we, too, need to be with people who suffer and rejoice.

Second, assuming that we have the good intention to treat everyone equally and well, we might believe that God is quite pleased with us. But who is represented by the *everyone* of our good intention? How outgoing and inclusive are we? How insular and protected? What determines or limits our encounters? Given the myriad incarnations or embodiments of God in the world, the more we encounter people different from ourselves, the more we will be enriched by continuing revelation. Let's examine this.

If we respond to people like ourselves, attempting to see God in them, the God we will find will be rather like ourselves. Thus our ideas of who God is—ideas that are inevitably narrow, prejudiced and limited—are supported. But the more we respond to people who are different from ourselves, attempting to let God shine through them, the more we will be surprised by the many faces of God. Our narrow, prejudiced notions will be seriously challenged!

Again, we may think of ourselves as reaching out to others, bringing compassion and godly enlightenment. If so, we cast them as recipients, ourselves as donors, and God as operating through us to them. Of course, God may do this. But, alternatively, we could think of ourselves as reaching out to others who are already embraced and touched by God. If so, we cast them as donors, ourselves as recipients, and God as operating through them to us. Then we will be amazed at God's versatility! But we can be both donor and recipient, bearer of God and receiver of God. Then we will be truly committed to the ministry that characterized Jesus, who not only brought healing love to others but who was frequently edified, nourished, by the faith and grace he encountered in them.

At the heart of Christian theology is the Incarnation. As the religion *par excellence* of embodiment, our religion should be characterized by an intense commitment to people and a real concern for those who suffer, who go hungry, or who are brutalized or abandoned. Sadly, it is not only those non-Christian religions which minimize suffering as illusory that tend to absolve themselves of responsibility for social change. Insofar as Christianity itself has failed to be as truly incarnational, it is also guilty of abandoning the needy of the world.

Christian ministry should become, quite explicitly, a means for building up the Body of Christ through the mutually enriching encounters of people who reflect the light of God into one another's eyes. Every single person will be enriched and God will be glorified, as more and more people experience the healing and reconciling presence of the Spirit of Christ. Saint Paul seems to speak of this, saying: "Everything is for your sake, so that grace, as it extends to more and more people, may increase thanksgiving, to the glory of God" (2 Cor 4:15). In every human encounter we can meet God. One of the greatest graces of a ministry that is truly cross-cultural is God's multifaceted self-revelation. So many faces of God! So much for us to absorb! It is certain that we will not emerge unchanged from the encounter. How might we facilitate it?

Tolerance of Our Self and Others

To revisit the pastoral style of Jesus is to rediscover a simple fact: in him mission, ministry, and love are embodied. This is profoundly important, even though rather obvious if we believe in the Incarnation. The words of Jesus, godly words, are not separated from healing touches and embraces. If we are to be Godly persons doing God's work, it will only be by making the embodied words of Jesus our own.

Jesus was deeply moved by the faith of foreigners and people shunned by the religiously pious. His understanding of the implications of his mission was affected by applying God's preferential option to such needy persons as he encountered their predicament.

Assuming our fundamental good will, how will we go about modifying our own pastoral style, in order to be caught up by God's Spirit? How will we endorse God's preferential option for the poor? First, a story, stark and tragic. Then a further look at our own approach to embodied ministry. Here is a reflection on the deaths of four American women missionaries:

I have several times watched the film Roses in December, *which shows the exhumation of these bodies. One can see clearly the limp figures in their jeans as they are hauled out of the grave with ropes. Time and again I have looked at Ita's body and thought this is what being a nun is about; this is about loving to the limit, about the grain of wheat falling to the ground and about the foolishness of those who follow Christ. There is a terrible purity in religious life when it is stripped of all the trappings of religion, of the self-consciousness and elitism.*

I think of the girl who told me she would not wear a sleeveless dress because she thought of Jesus as her fiance and he would not like it; and of a friend, who after six years in a convent, felt "immodest" in trousers. There is no modesty in being found dead in a river...and none in being raped in the back of a van by a bunch of brutal security guards—just a foolish identification with the suffering of the world and with the Son of God made man.

I find it very sad that Victorian prudery is confused with religious modesty and that the human body, its drives, and emotions, are not understood for what they are: the creations of an all-loving, all-powerful God. Only when we are helped to love ourselves and our bodies, to know ourselves as fundamentally good, will we be able to start loving each other as the Lord commanded (Cassidy, 1993:120–121).

Physical, Social, and Mystical Body

As we reflect on our Christian upbringing and current understanding of spirituality, can we claim to be comfortable friends with our bodies? Are we relaxed and at ease in our bodies? Or are we uncomfortable or embarrassed? Do we accept that our ministry is inseparable from the fact that we are embodied people, or do we minimize the importance of embodiment in our ministry?

"Body tolerance" is a cultural category which can help us understand people's ways of relating to their bodies, and indeed relating their bodies to the wider world. The notion of "high" or "low" body tolerance can be explanatory in a number of ways. They may be worth a brief look.

National Geographic magazine has shown us the people of Tahiti. The Tahitians of Captain Cook's day—or "South Sea Islanders" generally—typify people with high body tolerance. They present themselves as attractive people with attractive bodies. They appear open, expansive, relaxed, and sociable. In general, people with high body tolerance project and display their bodies without self-consciousness, and their physicality is a natural vehicle of communication, bonding, and reconciliation. This is not to suggest a link between loose morals and loose clothes, much less to identify a lack of morals with a lack of clothes. Natural modesty and a strong moral sense are often well developed among people with a high body tolerance. But some people with very high body tolerance seem to mock all conventions of social interaction. They appear lacking in modesty or respect for other people's boundaries and sensibilities. High body tolerance is relative and comes in many forms.

But if we contrast the cowled monk or wimpled nun, swathed in bland and formless clothing, eyes cast down, we see a very different picture. The stereotype, at least, identifies people with low body tolerance. They shun physical contact. They may deny the body, discipline it, or conceal it. Embrace and touch are not part of their repertoire of body language. They do not display, much less flaunt, their bodies. They are not necessarily without warmth or compassion, but it has to find expression despite, rather than through, their embodied selves.

Body tolerance is fairly simple notion, and anyone may attempt to identify themselves—or to check the impression made on friends—on a scale from very low to very high. But the wider implications are profound and of immediate relevance in the present context.

Members of a culture or subculture share many common traits and values. That is a defining characteristic of a culture. Consequently, within certain conventional limits, "people like ourselves" are highly likely to share our own level of body tolerance. One's own culture tends to standardize and generalize norms of acceptability, so that if someone should adopt a very different level of body tolerance such a person would either be shunned or would opt out.

Obviously there are many cultures, with many differences. And among the differences that distinguish any two cultures, the body tolerance quotient is often one of the most basic. Everyone knows implicitly that English and Italian men (stereotypically), or French and Russian girls (stereotypically), have very different ways of presenting their embodied selves. If the presentation of self is culturally meaningful (a kind of language), we must ask how people from different cultural backgrounds can encounter and communicate with one another. But if we identify embodiment as an essential feature of humanness, then the matter becomes particularly important when we look at it in the context of spirituality and ministry.

Questions immediately arise. Individually and culturally—and religiously—what determines body tolerance? What makes people more or less at ease with their embodied selves? How will people with different levels of body tolerance communicate? Will one particular body language dominate and become the vernacular? Such questions can be intriguing, even diverting, and produce a range of answers. But embodied Christians minister among other (and different) embodied persons, some of whom are not Christian. So what do we need to be aware of as we undertake interpersonal, even cross-cultural, embodied Christian ministry?

If the Christianity we have learned has contributed to our lack of ease with our bodies, how can we minister as Jesus ministered, as truly incarnate, human persons? If our body tolerance is very different from that of Jesus, how might we be called to adjust? We are called to reach out to others in the spirit of Jesus, and to be reachable by others. What if they have more respect for their bodies and embodiment than we do? We must do a better job in the future than has sometimes been done in the past. Otherwise, our attempts to "save souls" will fail to bear fruit. If our efforts are not directed to embodied human persons, they will fail to convince others that we preach a God who cares that we are inseparably, constitutionally, body as well as spirit.

What of the social body, the community? A pastoral strategy is required for all boundary-breaking Christians who try to read the clouds that gather wherever we minister. Since this might be one of the most important challenges we face, let us consider one more aspect of body tolerance (Douglas, 1970; Csordas, 1994). There is a remarkable correlation between how people relate to their own bodies on a personal level, and how their attitude is reflected at the broader social level: the individual body is a mirror of the social body.

If we are personally relaxed and tolerant, we will tend to be relaxed and tolerant at a social and cultural level. If we control and discipline our bodies, we may believe that a major responsibility of society is to exercise control and discipline. If there is some mutuality between the individual body and the social body, we might equally well begin from the other pole. Thus some people live in societies in which control and discipline are highly regarded, where boundaries are clearly marked, and where ambiguity is not tolerated. In such a social universe, personal regimentation and physical discipline, uniformity of dress, a clear distinction between sex roles, and a strenuous control over spontaneity, tend to characterize bodily behavior. But in a relaxed and open social world where ambiguity is tolerated and individual-ism is fostered, people will tend to be at ease in their bodies, de-monstrative and physical, and spontaneous.

Christians claim to be the Body of Christ (1 Cor 12:24). Theo-logically, we speak of the *Mystical Body*, but we are both alive and human. So our final question concerns *how* we might present ourselves as Christ's body on earth? If people live in a Christian social environment where the church is understood as a "perfect society," there will be a place for everything and everything will be put in its place. Control, clarity, purity, and certainty will be major social virtues. There will be little tolerance of ambiguity, experimentation, or spontaneity in ritual or discipline. And with the help of training and a system of rewards and punishments, individuals will conform and cohere. A strong, dogmatic com-munity will result. But its survival depends on the maintenance of conformity, the patrolling of boundaries, and the imposition of punishments. In the end, it will not be experimental, will re-sist being ecumenical, and will favor intellect over embodiment. It will inevitably fossilize.

A *purity code* characterizes religious systems that are very con-cerned about their boundaries. We saw this briefly in the chapter on cultural and cultic attitudes in ancient Israel. A *purity code* will pass judgment on matters of ambiguity and messiness, and will effectively clarify and resolve them. But human beings are, in fact, messy—from the moment of birth onwards. Denial of that is a denial of human embodiment. And denial of human incarnation is an insult to the Word made flesh and to God who made us in God's very image and likeness.

Consequently, attempts to legislate ways in which human be-ings are allowed to be human and express their affectivity and fundamental humanness will become artificial or unnatural and will always sit uneasily with a religion of Incarnation. The use of moral force to resolve ambiguity or to control authentic human outreach will always harm real people. Jesus experienced this in his outreach to those on the margins, when opposed by the keepers of the law and upholders of the purity code.

If human embodiment is respected, bodily boundaries and apertures are also respected—not simply for exclusion, refusal, or elimination but for absorption, embrace, and honest intercourse. A balance must be found, but not inflexibly maintained. Intake and output are equally important, both attesting to healthy functioning. But where there is excessive emphasis on grooming and purifying, eliminating and excluding, disciplining and controlling, at the expense of some messiness and looseness, some embracing and including, there is great danger that our embodied selves are not being respected and nurtured. And this becomes sinful.

Not only have Christians struggled to do justice to the integrated persons they are, they have sometimes projected their own Manichaean, dualistic self-understanding upon others (Miles, 1990:1). Where they have successfully transferred such behaviors on to people of other cultures, they have sometimes trampled on long-accumulated local wisdom about how to live in the body realistically and with dignity. There is surely room for us to be more open to the multifarious ways of being human, and to learn how God can be part of human communities that are less obsessive, less neurotic, and less guilt-ridden about their bodies than are some Christian communities. Above all, we can look again at how Jesus celebrated his own humanness: in and through the Incarnation, the embodiment of God.

Jesus, Embodiment of Pastoral Care

Jesus lived within in a restrictive religious environment. Boundaries were patrolled, rules were multiplied, punishments were harsh, intolerance was widespread. Purification codes excluded the sinful: the messy, the impure, those whose bodily conditions were less than perfect. In this religious environment, exclusion was effectively permanent, and the excluded were thus deprived of hope.

God became a human being, incarnated in Jesus whose pastoral response was to take the initiative, to reach out, to touch, to cross boundaries, to include, to forgive, and to extend healing and hope. He refused to be cowed by rules which threatened him with contamination and pollution, or to apologize for his physical limitations and needs. He spoke intimately of God, and proclaimed that God loves the imperfect in body, and that God's healing is intended to restore and to raise up those who are destroyed or abased. He refused to be paralyzed by fear.

Women and children were religiously marginal. Jesus not only sought them out and embraced them, but called his followers to be as socially powerless as they were. People whose lives were contaminated by bodily impurity, physical defect, or occupational messiness (menstruating women, lepers, prostitutes, or tax collectors) were not only befriended but explicitly assured they would be the first in God's kingdom (Mt 21:31–32). Those who were simply invisible (the hungry, the thirsty, the naked, the sick, the imprisoned, the strangers) were dignified by being identified with Christ himself (Mt 25:35ff). Furthermore, Jesus asserted that nothing that touches a person can pollute or contaminate, for sinful pollution comes only from within (Mk 7:14). Human persons can pollute, but bodies cannot be polluted.

Not surprisingly, given this attitude, Jesus was frequently confronted with his disciples' paralyzing fear: what about the establishment? As Jesus gathered people around him, he needed constantly to encourage them not to be afraid. Fear appeared to be the greatest single factor preventing true discipleship. It was also symptomatic of lack of faith. But the ministry of Jesus touched the disciples' fear, for it was a healing ministry and it demanded a new understanding of humanness and human contact. So fear of physical illness and spiritual contamination needed to be overcome if the disciples were to become the kind of ministers Jesus needed them to be.

Are we not a little indecisive and fearful? We are called to transcend paralyzing fear, to move beyond isolation, and to be healed. Then, as healed healers, we can join the ministry of inclusion and reconciliation. Part of our fear may be that even if we prepared to relearn how to be at ease in our embodiment, we might be criticized and ridiculed or condemned. But Jesus invites us to a healing *community,* and community is where people learn, together, what is appropriate and life-giving. No matter how old we may be, or how wise, Jesus wants to teach us something new. That demands not just intellectual assent but an embodied response: movement, change, risk. We need not fear contamination nor compromise. Have faith, do not be afraid, trust: these are the watchwords. Then we can touch and gather and find new communities.

Jesus—who reached out, embraced, touched, and was touched by others—is portrayed as someone at ease with himself: he had a high body tolerance. He was not controlled by fear or by human respect, but trusted his own instincts and intuitions. He was truly incarnate—so human indeed, as to be a scandal to those who could not accept that God's power was at work in him.

If we are to be more like Jesus, we must imitate him not only in his divinity but in his humanness. Jesus starts by loving; he proceeds by loving; he concludes by loving. Jesus loves people, human beings, embodied persons. In his daily ministry Jesus fulfills the promise of Isaiah (40:3–4; cf: Lk 3:6) that "all flesh will see the salvation of God." Our spirituality and our pastoral witness must be both incarnational and responsive to humanness of others, or it fails to do what Jesus did and therefore it fails to be authentic spirituality or true pastoral care.

Chapter Seven

Growing in Age and Wisdom

Whoever carries over into the afternoon the law of morning must pay for it with damage to [the] soul.

CARL GUSTAV JUNG

The heart of the old is always young in two things, in love for the world and length of hope.

MOHAMMED

Illness was identification with the Crucifixion. We should not be misled by modern notions. When the [medieval] woman sought illness as fact and as metaphor, it was a fully active fusing with the death agonies of Christ.

CAROLYN WALKER BYNUM

Sex, Sickness, and Senescence

The sociologist Max Weber (1864–1920) coined a useful phrase: an *ideal type* is a way of representing a class of persons or things so as to identify standard or typical features. An ideal type is an abstraction. Actual people or things are more nuanced and more idiosyncratic. In this chapter, references to parishes or Western culture are references to ideal types.

Many people today find it difficult to speak about contemporary Western culture in any unitary way. Whatever it may be, it is certainly suffering a crisis of identity and meaning. Half a century ago, Viktor Frankl identified this as the great malaise of the modern age. Western culture appears deeply ambivalent about three issues that concern Christians directly, and each one is critically important to the functioning of society and individuals. Unless a more wholesome attitude is adopted, the culture will continue to contribute to its own breakdown. The three issues are these: first, sex and sexuality; second, sickness or illness; and third, growing old, or age itself. After looking briefly at the first two, we will consider the third in greater detail.

Unfortunately and with grave consequences, in the Christian West, these three social realities have been widely treated as abnormal. As a result, incalculable damage has been done. But they have not always and universally been treated as abnormal. If we retrieve the wisdom that they are potentially functional, creative, and godly, perhaps we can be enriched and reach for the transcendence to which God's grace calls us. The alternative is to flounder through avoidance or denial.

Christianity, Sexuality, and Women

"I believe in the resurrection of the body," declares the Apostles' Creed. In Great Britain the Marriage Service still contains this profoundly beautiful formula: "With this ring, I thee wed. This gold and silver I thee give. *With my body I thee worship.* And with all my worldly goods I thee endow." But sexuality has not fared well in Christian circles. The original tradition was distorted, poisoned by systems that opposed mind to body, spirituality to sexuality, and man to woman.

Man and woman are made in God's image, which God declared a very good thing (Gen 1:31). But over time, Christian *men* decided this image was to be found in human rationality rather than human embodiment. Christ's humanity came to be inferred, not through his maleness as such but through his birth from a human mother. A body was not considered adequate evidence of respectable humanity. Furthermore, men argued that women were hardly rational, therefore not human (Miles, 1989:121). Only at the Council of Trent (1545–1563) was the contrary thesis affirmed. Nevertheless, in the succeeding centuries, ecclesiastical suspicion or fear of sexuality has not disappeared.

There is, however, another interesting part to the story, another strand even in the Christian tradition. In the *Letter to Diognetus* of the mid-second century, Christians are described as proudly embodied:

For how can it be anything but unlawful to receive some of the things created by God for the use of [humanity]…and to reject others as if useless? And what does it deserve but ridicule to be proud of mutilation of the flesh as proof of election, as if [this made people] especially beloved of God. Jesus came "as a human being to human beings." God is "kind to [humanity]…and free from wrath and true, and he alone is good" (Quasten, 1948).

In Jesus, God identifies intimately with us. And though this does not make us sinless it does indicate that we are not reducible to, or demeaned by, either embodiment or sexuality. Originally, to follow an incarnate Christ meant that naked embodiment, including sexuality, had religious meaning (Miles, 1989). When nakedness implied vulnerability, original sin was rarely reduced to sexuality. Into the fifth century, naked baptism was standard. Cyril of Jerusalem enthused: "Marvelous! You were naked in the sight of all and were not ashamed! Truly you bore the image of the first-formed Adam, who was naked in the garden and 'was not ashamed'" (Miles, 1989:33). There can be no authentic human holiness, much less holy sexuality, unless we first remember that our embodiment is one of the ways we image God. Often we have forgotten.

In spite of amnesia, respect for embodied sexuality did not entirely die. It flowered again in the Renaissance, "The first and last phase of Christian art that can claim full Christian orthodoxy…the first Christian art in a thousand years to confront the Incarnation entire, upper and lower body together, not excluding even the body's sexual component" (Steinberg, 1984: 141). Jesus is represented in anatomical detail, an explicit illustration of the doctrine of the Incarnation. "To profess that God once embodied himself in a human nature is to confess that the eternal, there and then, became human and sexual.…The evidence of Christ's sexual member serves as a pledge of God's humanation" (Steinberg, 1984:142). "Christ redeems not only our physiological differences as men and women; he redeems our sexual nature (if not our sexual acts) as well" (Bynum, 1992:84).

Nevertheless, ambiguity has characterized sexuality for Christians generally. Medieval women were associated with body, both negatively (because of its association with sexuality) and positively (because of their likeness to Jesus' mother, Mary). Even Jesus, fully human and male, was also spoken of both as mother and as female (Bynum, 1982; 1992). But ominously, in Christendom, ambiguity tended to degenerate into the demonization of sexuality, particularly women's. This is not true Christianity, but a cultural expression of patriarchy and clericalism.

Patriarchal cultures feed on control, especially of women. An easy ploy is to treat women as anomalous or grotesque (Miles,

1989:145–168). Patriarchal power-playing or social control has shown itself in domination over women's bodies. They were to be confined, enclosed, and controlled by men. Uncontrolled bodies were caricatured in women who wore men's clothing, and in the whore: unconfined, loose, uncontrolled people were *therefore* ungodly, and "threatening the very order and stability of society itself" (Miles, 1989:166).

What specifically Christian insight might rehabilitate human sexuality? Sexual *relationship* implies some surrender of control and some sharing of vulnerability; otherwise sexuality becomes egotistical, dominating, or violent: less than human. Making love also invites mutuality and reconciliation, "grist for the mill of spiritual life, for transform[ation]" (Westley, 1994). But a church in control will be a church whose controllers cannot afford to be vulnerable or mutual in this way! A church which tries to exercise control, and to exert control over sexual relationships, will soon become repressive. Sexuality will be demeaned and regarded as "abnormal"; lifelong celibacy (or dutiful and procreative rather than pleasurable and recreational sex) will become the implicit norm. Thus is fashioned the distorting lens through which others' lives are scrutinized and judged.

We are not called to follow the pathologies of any culture, including those of a nominally Christian culture; the life and teachings of Jesus are the norm. He became as we are in everything but sin (Phil 2:7–8), and sexuality is not sin. Therefore is it not abnormal. Too often the church is experienced as disembodied, disdainful of the world's body and human bodies—and not only sexual bodies but broken, hungry, wounded, abused, unwanted, and unloved bodies. But as human beings we are called to make (a world of) love. The chief command of Jesus was that we should love wholeheartedly (Mt 22:37). People should discover God through their bodies, and that discovery includes their sexual lives. That is the implication of claiming that experience shapes theology rather than vice versa. How else shall we meet God? If, like Jesus, we accept our bodies, our sexual differentiation, and our sexuality, using them appropriately, then God is glorified in us and we are humanized. The religion Jesus preached and embodied was counter-cultural and prophetic. In every time and place, disciples are challenged to be faithful to Jesus, to live in tension with merely cultural understandings, whether of hierarchy or sexuality.

Christianity's central project is based on God's becoming an enfleshed human person in Jesus. Respecting our human nature and the divine plan of salvation, that project is to transform us, not by repudiating who we are but by gratefully acknowledging and understanding its meanings. This can only be brought about by deep respect for the actual situation in which each person is encountered. Concluding a brilliant book on the subject, Margaret Miles judges that in Christianity

the flesh has largely been scorned, the body marginalized, in the project of a "spiritual" journey. [But] Christian doctrinal affirmation of human bodies is unambiguous; doctrines of creation, the incarnation of Christ, and the resurrection of the body clearly posit a faith in which bodies are integral (Miles, 1989:185).

The reason for the marginalization of the flesh "was the sexism of Christian societies." Christian practice "fatally undermined the Christian project of integrating the flesh....Christian societies effectively ghettoized the flesh, undermining even the strongest doctrinal ratifications of 'the body'" (Miles, *loc. cit.*). By making abnormal what God made holy, Christianity drove one wedge between individuals and their bodies, and another between God and God's image.

III-At-Ease With Pain and Disease

To identify physical sickness with moral decay (Sontag, 1989) is to see it only as pathological and abnormal. The sick of Jesus' day were identified with the sinful. In a rich irony, Jesus declared he had come especially for them (Lk 5:31–32). If the physician comes for the less-than-perfect, then each of us may take comfort in our special calling! We are not perfect because we are not God. But we do aspire to being "on the Way." To the Christian, suffering, pain, and sickness are not irredeemably evil. On the contrary: by sharing our sufferings Jesus sanctified them. What *is* evil is the denial of suffering, if it makes us impervious through drug-induced oblivion, or insensitive because we forget we are part of a suffering, bleeding, broken world. We should be disturbed by the way illness is treated in Western culture and in many communities.

A culture confused about life itself is likely to treat sickness as unnatural or anomalous. But shunning or denial will never produce enlightenment. Many cultures possess the wisdom that sickness-with-healing (not curing!) is both natural and a way of transcendence, a path to the supernatural. We have seen examples.

New Age gurus promise wholeness if not painlessness. They lie. Even as we Christians support wholesome healing, we must "re-cognize" the inevitability of suffering and death. They are normal. Pain is part of life, and a pain-free culture would be a lie and an injustice based on denial and privilege. The privileged individual may mask the pain and disregard the wider community. But we are social creatures, existing in relationship. Pain and suffering are part of society. Nor can we have a pain-free spirituality; because spirituality is not focused on or controlled by self alone, because pain can be redemptive, and because we are the Body of Christ which is still crucified and bleeding in our brothers and sisters.

A culture dependent on life-extending and death-dealing technologies will create a world of virtual reality. People then lose touch with real life, which includes the pain of birthing and dying. Societies less dependent on technologies may be better able to live with these realities. Sufferers always search for meaning, but meaning resides and is to be discovered in community, rather than individuals. We saw it in the !Kung, the Nigerian scapegoat, and the dispossessed in Darwin. We should also be able to see it in the community we call church (Marty, 1994). If not, we must make meaning together.

Medieval women, forever told they were "only" material and their men were rational, made a virtue out of a social reality, and came closer to their Savior and their fellow sufferers (Bynum, 1987). They reached God not by reversing roles but by sinking more deeply into them. The more saintly among them interpreted illness and suffering as a special grace and as participation in the Crucifixion, actively identifying themselves with Christ. Suffering in patience (the virtue of longanimity) was the commonest attribute of women saints (53 percent) between A.D. 1000 and 1700. Offered on behalf of the community and for the redemption of others, suffering was experienced as identification with and imitation of Christ (Bynum, 1992:48,60,131,189).

What of ourselves? If we are committed to the poor and needy, and moving to the margins, we will encounter some of the languages of pain and suffering, sickness and death. It is important to recall that although some suffering and sickness may be normal, there is also great injustice and inequity if a society's complacency with its members' distress has become the accepted norm. Our responsibility is to stand fast (like medieval women or the !Kung), to help carry the burden of pain. Our calling is to love and to develop an appetite for justice in the context of suffering and death. We, together, are the Body of Christ, dying and rising. "The suffering of one is the suffering of all, and the suffering of all is part of each" (Kollar, 1990:215). We are not alone, for Christ suffers in and with and for us. But unless our spirituality is grounded in our responsiveness to the needs of others, we still have a long way to go.

Pain is not simply to be endured, much less, passively. Suffering, concretely—in embodied, pain-filled people—can become a sacrament to sacralize us all. It has the potential to build up community and help us live amid chaos and ambiguity, to assist our growth in the Spirit. If raw pain is simply a component of the physical aspect of life, suffering is pain transmuted under the influence of hope and in the direction of transcendence. Unless transmuted or redeemed, it can destroy. But the person of faith and hope will survive (Heb 11:1–3). Disciples and ministers of outreach, we Christians must be sufferers if we are to commit ourselves to real people in the real world. Any proposal which seems to avoid or escape pain is trying to avoid or escape our humanness and its responsibilities. Pain should not be glorified, and "bad pain is bad pain and must be dealt with as we deal with any evil" (Kollar, 1990:213): but it is to be transcended.

For a Christian there is no easy solution. There must be commitment for the long haul. But the task is not beyond ordinary people. What is most needed is commitment to those ordinary supportive and nurturing roles which women have traditionally and heroically undertaken. None of us can heal everything. Christianity might be more credible if it were less bombastic and grandiose in its claims to have all the answers (Marty, 1994:230–231). What we can do is pledge ourselves. We can love. We can read the clouds. And amid the inevitable and normal pain and suffering, we will, Jesus reliably informs us, find peace.

A contemporary Christian spirituality must be a one of solidarity with our changing world. Jesus is our example, the finest representative of humanity. In his life, death, and even in Resurrection he was part of the community, and committed to creating and fostering community. Yet Christianity is no retirement community for comfortable living, and it should relativize every culture it meets. Every cultural knee must bow before the amazing challenge of community envisaged by Jesus. Christianity is thus called to be a counter-culture, and should inspire its members to live lives to the full, as Jesus Christ did. Pastoral caregivers of all kinds are typical bearers of these signs. They continue the legacy of medieval women who saw illness as a lived metaphor for union with Christ, and as an opportunity for solidarity among the community of believers. And each of us, committed to cross-cultural ministry, must be counter-cultural in the presence of illness. A truly missionary commitment will not only show us or remind us of the pervasive extent of illness: it will simply not allow us to forget.

The Face of Age

Assuming we are trying to integrate our sexuality, and our experiences of sickness, with our spirituality, there remains a final question for everyone searching for growth rather than stagnation, activity rather than passivity: how will we advance in grace and wisdom as we inevitably advance in age? Perhaps better put, how will we continue to respond to our own call to conversion, and resist the temptation either to claim that there is nothing much more for us to do, or to think it is time for our spirituality to relapse into some kind of retirement?

For women born in 1900 in the United States, the life expectancy was 46; for men, 45 (Friedan, 1993). In England, it was about 47 and 44, respectively. English women born in 2000 will have a life-expectancy of 79.4; for men 74.1 (*Guardian Weekly*, Jan. 25, 1998:24); figures for the United States are almost identical. Of all the people who ever lived, only those alive today can expect as much as half a lifetime after the years of childbearing and rearing (Friedan, 1993). This is nothing less than a social and cultural revolution.

What does this mean for disciples of Christ, those who bring good news in his name? Pondering the "extra" thirty years or more that citizens of the rich nations may expect to enjoy (an increase of more than 60 percent on one's life span), the parable of the Talents comes to mind (Mt 25:14–30). What does God expect of us? What is our moral and social obligation in this novel situation? And how can we forget the central challenge and paradox of our faith: "Those who want to save their lives will lose it; and those who lose their life for my sake, and for the sake of the gospel, will save it. For what will it profit them to gain the whole world and forfeit their life? Indeed, what can they give in return for their life?" (Mk 8:35–37). "To save one's life means to hold onto it, to love it and be attached to it and therefore to fear death" (Nolan, 1992:139). It also implies a failure to take up one's cross and follow Jesus.

The unprecedented opportunities created by this extension of life offer a challenge to all. But there is also a great danger that they will be used selfishly or squandered. Christians particularly, should be sensitive and responsible, using the blessings of life for the benefit of many, as good stewards and lovers. Lest we overlook our obligations, and the opportunities for good, here are five points to ponder.

The Meaning of Life

The universal human lot is to be born, to grow, to age, and to die, but each human society must make meaning out of this biological pattern. Social meaning, as distinct from individual meaning, may be discovered by extending the biological and social context of an individual's life, and then drawing some conclusions. A person is not reducible to a monad (an isolated, independent individual); however, not every person is a robust adult. Socially defined, a person exists before birth and after death. That existence depends on a particular network of changing relationships, a social context. So important is this context that an individual cut off from community may cease to be a person in any meaningful way. In short, the biologically individuated human being becomes a bearer of meaning, largely in terms of the community to which he or she belongs.

This notion may be unfamiliar to people of the rich and specialized nations. We are perfectly capable of reducing or making abstraction of the context and considering the autonomous individual in isolation. This will inevitably affect the meaning we attribute to persons. The Western world typically considers the individual as self-contained, self-motivated, and self-serving ("so long as I'm not harming anyone…"). Western culture has been quite successful in separating social and individual meaning, and promoting the cult of the individual. Many people are persuaded that the meaning of their lives is measured by personal achievements, often judged not alongside others' but in comparison to or in competition with them. "Success" means achievements noticed or recognized by a competitive society. Death is the inevitable conclusion to a successful life.

What of people of the Incarnation and Resurrection? For us, meaning is construed within a community of faith. For us, life should be lived in the context of a community broader than the biological family. For us the worth of a life is measured by how well we have loved God and neighbor. Reflecting on insights gleaned from our life-experience of faith, culture, and ministry, we should be able to draft a plan of pastoral action based on the particular meanings of Christian life.

Naming the Lies

Before we can identify a specifically Christian meaning for life, two lies must be exposed. They are propagated by, and inseparable from, the dominant cultures in which many of us live. Their implications are contrary to the values of Jesus. The first proclaims that aging is tantamount to the disintegration and decline of the person. The second declares that aging is abnormal and therefore to be resisted.

The cultures that tell these lies have built upon the sand. In their cult of youthful individualism they have claimed that the peak of human creativity is reached somewhere around the fortieth year, and is followed by marked, inevitable, and universal decline. A consequence has been a culturally conditioned fear, chronological or biological. Fortieth birthdays, midlife crises, and menopause have been the focus of massive attention, and whole industries and technologies have been marshaled in an effort to mask or delay these feared messengers of human decline and increasing worthlessness. Measurable physical decline and signs of age have been equated with mental decline which, in turn, is equated with approaching death and annihilation. Add the proliferation of specialized healthcare, the technical capacity to prolong vital functions in traumatized bodies, and the near-idolatrous cult of self-indulgent youth, and what has been produced? A dis-eased society characterized by an inability to live and a refusal to die (Nuland, 1993).

So long as death is perceived as unnatural or abnormal, medical technology will strive to postpone it for longer and longer. But medical science will never prevent death, because people are not immortal. The prolongation of vital signs is no indicator of the extension of meaningful life, however defined. If the extension of life inhibits people's realistic preparation for death, then it contributes to the dehumanization of society. If life-support systems replace death-preparation systems, then both our Christian faith and our pastoral care have proven inadequate for their tasks.

Two Faces of Age

The third point builds on the ruins of the two lies. Cross-culturally, age has very different faces. One face appears depressed, and is either self-absorbed or pathetically trying to stave off the signs of physical decline. Behind this face is a person treated by society as dispensable if not already obsolete and worthless, and increasingly frustrated or enraged at the inability to become immortal. This is *the weak face of age.* The other face belongs to a dignified figure, notably past physical perfection, but mellowing and growing in wisdom, and embraced by a community that knows the precious worth of this special person. This is *the strong face of age.* If ours is to be the strong face, then we must seek it and claim it, for it will not come upon us automatically.

The weak face of age marks people who fall victim to the self-fulfilling prophecy of age as decline and despair; their self-esteem crumbling even as wrinkles caress their skin. Clinging to the past or to fleeting youth, they always think the aged are other people, never themselves. They can become truly lamentable if they fail to live appropriately. Anyone who believes that the best is in the past has already lost hope. That is no way for a follower of Jesus to behave. Not only will such people fail to break through into the new world of age, they will make themselves ill. One face of mental illness in aging people is fearfulness of the passage of time. This is indicated by avoidance of life-giving novel events and situations (Friedan, 1993:119).

The strong face of age is very different. The ability graciously to let go of youth and to mature into age is the sign of one's capacity to be enriched and enrich others at the fountain of age.

The golden years bring golden opportunities. But only those who do not cling to the past and who balance risk with prudence will be able to meet the challenge of a lifetime. In order to break through to the strong face of age, it is important to nurture and maintain relationship to persons and places, and to a mutually supportive community. Isolation is as much the enemy of successful aging as is mindless conformity. Deterioration results from a diet of routine and nostalgia, more than from chronological age. The evidence for productive growth in the "extra" third of life is overwhelming. Those who cope, grow; and the potential growth is truly amazing and varied: emotional and spiritual, intellectual and moral. These years may offer the opportunity to move from the achievement of self-actualization to the wisdom of authentic transcendence.

For Christians, growth in wisdom, age, and grace (cf. Lk 2:40) is a familiar phrase. It should also be a familiar experience. Studies prove what Christianity indicates: chronological growth is only one sign of humanness or fulfillment. If Jesus grew not only in age but in wisdom and grace, so may we. Age is part of a curve of continued development in the human person, a development not limited to physical vigor but inclusive of moral and spiritual strength. The God who leads is the God who invites us not to cling to a part of life, nor to fear death, but to receive life in its abundance (Jn 10:10) and to live it to the full. This, of course, is inseparable from sharing it with others and with laying it down, and from taking up the cross and following Jesus.

Life-Enhancing Crossover

Women outlive men, particularly in the rich nations. In a dominant patriarchal culture in which women have been widely deprived and men privileged, one might expect men to live longer but they do not. What could this mean? Generally, men are more aggressively competitive, more independent-spirited, and far less adaptable and open to change than women. Despite women's traditionally circumscribed roles and high mortality in childbirth, they still outlived men at the beginning of the twentieth century. At its end, women's life expectancy is about eight years greater than men's, and the gap continues to widen. The fastest-growing age group in the United States and the world is women over 85. Far more males than females die each year in the same decade of their age. The suicide rate for men aged 65 is about 35 per 100,000; among the over-85s, it has risen to 62. Women's suicide is only a tenth of men's, and among women over 85 the rate actually declines (Friedan, 1993:134–5;175).

American men appear to be less good at living than American women. This could be because they are not taught the necessary skills or techniques. Is it also because they lack the necessary wisdom? Living is a process which must be learned if persons and societies are to flourish, prosper, and grow wise. Similarly, dying. But in a culture which fears and denies death, people will have little or no expertise at dying. Not surprisingly, perhaps, physicians and clergy are among the very worst people when it comes to *ars moriendi,* knowing how to die.

One priceless quality for those who would grow into vital age, is "crossover," whereby a person learns to integrate the masculine and feminine sides. When sexual competitiveness is no longer required, we may bring forth a hidden or repressed dimension of our humanness, which is life-enhancing and prolonging. A cross-cultural study discovered that in later years

the man can claim his feminine side, which had. to be repressed to allow him to protect his young as warrior; the woman can reclaim her assertive, aggressive, masculine side, which had to be repressed for her to stay close to the young she must nurture. Now, in reclaiming and integrating their suppressed masculine and feminine sides, these elders play a larger parental role that helps to keep the whole tribe human, and the species to survive (Gutman in Friedan, 1993: 86).

Such evidence suggests an evolutionary value in "crossover." But a society which strongly disapproves of male affectivity and vulnerability will not encourage it. According to a recent study of the United States, as women age they are characterized by flexibility, excitement, and increased pride, showing a decrease of fear, anger, and depression, and an increase in self-esteem and general happiness. Significantly, there is a greater adaptability to spousal death. And when that major transition has been dealt with, women show an ability to live in harmony with their bodies, even in ill-health, continually renewing themselves, sharing vulnerability and moving to transcendence in a way quite unmatched by most men. For women, widowhood and age offer a further stage of growth, embodying some of the characteristic strengths of men.

By contrast, men, trained as independent and less comfortable with affectionate intimacy or the sharing of vulnerability, do not fare well. Clinging to competitiveness and independence, they are less suited to forming new communities and discovering new, "feminine" ways of living. The "bonus" of several decades has not yet been as well received by men as by women.

Could the new permission for men to soften their macho image and open themselves up to emotionality, tenderness and intimacy give them those new years of age that women, but not men, enjoy today? The competitive orientation toward achievement and dominance is increasingly maladaptive, incongruous, even dangerous, especially for older men. Flexibility in response to the discontinuities, uncontrollable changes, and exigencies of life so long experienced by women now emerges as an essential strength in age, for men as well as women (Friedan, 1993:168–9).

Appropriate Spirituality

Jung insisted that we should not try to live the "afternoon of life" by the "chart of the morning." The gradual decline of physical strength brings a new agenda or allows us to complete the old. It is a time very suited to things of the spirit: the neglected inner life may be nurtured. There is everything to be gained and little to be lost by achieving the integrity of age: it is the failure to do so that "leads to despair, vindictiveness, depression, suicide, or a deep fear of old age and death" (Friedan, 1993:122).

According to Freud, love and work are two essential ingredients of productive age. These fit very well with the idea of a God who leads, and with the notion of continuous and never-ending conversion. If the ability to modify old goals and create new ones is a measure of successful aging, then we are challenged to discover new forms of community and new ways of loving that will build up the Body of Christ, even as our own bodies grow weaker. Jesus says "learn from me; for I am gentle and humble in heart, and you will find rest for your souls" (Mt 11:29). It is not necessary to be physically strong, youthful, or aggressive; it may be necessary for some of us to learn gentleness and meekness.

A spirituality of perfection may be both unhelpful and scandalous if it tries to make us who we are not. We are not God. Nor, by sheer effort, can we make ourselves as pleasing to God as we might be impressive to others. That is heresy. True perfectibility is about cooperating with God's transforming grace. Our job is to bring grace to birth in ourselves and one another, not as an initiative but as a response; not privately but socially (2 Cor 4:13–15). A misplaced spirituality of perfection may lead us to aspire to being invincible. That may be youthful conceit. But youth is not as prized in other societies as it is in our own. What is important is wisdom; and wisdom, if it comes at all, comes with age. The wise are declining in body as they grow in grace. So, precisely insofar as we age with grace, we may have special credibility: there is no need for denial or deceit.

The Evolutionary Significance of Longevity

Personal piety or spirituality divorced from a community (the Body of Christ) is not yet Christian and certainly not missionary. What remains to be done therefore?

The experience of aging may be particularly suited to a counter-cultural proclamation of the gospel in today's culture, for at least two reasons. Someone has to stand against the fiction of age as inevitable decline and unproductivity. But, further, the precious gift of years must not be used selfishly when so many of our brothers and sisters are in such pain and suffering such injustice: "From everyone to whom much has been given, much will be required; and from the one to whom much has been entrusted, even more will be demanded" (Lk 12:42).

Are we learning to use the years well? Will humanity—the family of nations and of people across the globe—be better off for the extra years given to the privileged few? How will we use our time to become better ministers, better missionary Christians? These are timely questions. This chapter was begun on the author's fifty-fifth birthday—already a bonus decade beyond other people's life expectancy. If the extra "age" of our own lifetime might be as important as the age of childhood for our ongoing humanization, then in evolutionary terms it is not to be used selfishly. We should probably search for its meaning in the context of God's Providence.

What if, in terms of Divine Providence, the *telos* or purpose of the extra years is to bring about some kind of biblical *Jubilee:*

a radical change, reversal, and remission of accumulated debt? What if, in conformity with the Divine Plan, some people would undertake to share their lives with those whose quality of life was particularly low: to make a preferential option for the poor? What if some Christians from the richer nations were galvanized into using their extra years explicitly to alleviate sickness and injustice? We might never know, until the Last Judgement, whether this is an intended purpose of extended lives, but we do know two things from our scriptural tradition. We know that when the Son of humanity comes in glory, he will say to those on his right:

Come, you whom my Father has blessed, take for your heritage the kingdom prepared for you since the foundation of the world. For I was hungry and you gave me food; I was thirsty and you gave me drink; I was a stranger and you made me welcome; naked and you clothed me, sick and you visited me, in prison and you came to see me (Mt 25:31–37);

and furthermore, we know that the greatest commandment is to love one's neighbor as oneself (Mt 22:39), and that "*there is no greater love than to lay down your life for your friend*" (Jn 15:13–14). What if we took these sayings and images very seriously indeed, and glimpsed a real purpose and potential in the time we have remaining?

So much for thoughts about the evolutionary significance of longevity. But there is another perspective—that of the young and active among a "graying" population. How might they respond and relate to their senior brothers and sisters?

"People of age" are neither dispensable nor replaceable. Whatever treasures or wisdom they have gathered might be lost if not passed on. But unless there are recipients, it matters little that there are donors. In the contemporary West, the younger generations may be in the process of losing vital wisdom by belittling and marginalizing their aging members. Somehow, therefore, youth and age must strive to pull together. Otherwise communities and cultures will be destroyed.

It is a sociological fact that cross-culturally, marginal people—including perhaps the elderly and physically weak—have insights that can be life-giving and critical to people of the center and the mainstream. If such people are demeaned or ostracized, those at the center may remain safe, but they are also culturally and spiritually impoverished (Gittins, 1998: Ch 5).

The senior generation may be in a marginal position. Growing old is itself a *liminal* experience, challenging and dangerous yet carrying great potential. If its members risk a little and approach the more youthful openhandedly, and with the flexibility of which they are capable, they might be received and welcomed to the great enrichment of all.

Older Christians should have a particular legacy of their own: unwavering faith, undaunted hope, abiding love. Where there is a vision of Jesus the Christ, an active engagement with one's own unfinished story, and a community to love, there the Christian is a powerful witness to life. To say that such people and such attitudes cannot change the world is to be blind and deaf, as well as terminally cynical.

Conversion is never a purely private affair: it is conversion *from* and conversion *to*, and as such is relational. The second half of life, which Jung saw as particularly suited to conversion, is particularly conducive to a deepening and a widening of relationships. To people who have never stopped moving to the margins and seeking the lost and wounded, there may be a wonderful potential for ongoing conversion. It is simply not true, as a certain school of psychology and spirituality would have us believe, that by about one's fiftieth year "we complete the work of dismantling the last false assumption, and live with a sense of having completed something, a sense that we are whoever we are going to be" (Gould, 1987:310). If this were so, God has given some of us years or decades of useless life! How could that possibly square with a world in such need of compassionate commitment?

We recall that Jesus urged people to read the signs of the times. Each of us must attend to this. Each one must learn how to lose the life we want to save, and to cling to the life that is not passing away. Each of us must live courageously in conformity with the gospel. For those not yet of a "certain age," perhaps some of the thoughts discussed here will provide encouragement for their future agenda and apostolate. For those already in the afternoon of life and committed to the Christian pilgrimage, may they at least be a mark of solidarity, a token of affirmation, and perhaps an instrument of grace.

Afterword

Signs of the Times

Through the globalization of markets and communications' technologies, the contemporary world has become highly accessible. Even from its remoter parts, CNN and other satellite news programs are available. We can see virtually everywhere, visually and televisually, and increasing millions of us are highly mobile. The more mobile and financially secure of us are also among the first generations on earth who can expect to live for seven or eight decades and to maintain a quality of life that is the envy of millions.

The twin opportunities of mobility and longevity can be a means of grace. Christians are invited to become neither interlopers nor tourists but disciples who engage with the world as "good-news-ers." We encounter other people, neither with empty hands nor full of self-importance but in the spirit of Jesus—a spirit of true humility. Jesus went to bring faith and to seek faith, to encounter and to be encountered, to show people God's amazing plans and to be amazed by God's activity in the people he met.

To the slow-witted, Jesus was a teacher, calling people to pay attention and to understand (cf. Lk 24:25). Not only did he call them to read the clouds, he painstakingly showed them how to.

But some were petulant and cynical and self-righteous, and others asked him questions in order to trap him or scoff. Saint Mark's Gospel, tellingly, is unambiguous and uncompromising: "[They] came and began arguing with him, asking him for a sign from heaven, to test him. And he sighed deeply in his spirit and said, 'Why does this generation ask for a sign? Truly I tell you, no sign will be given this generation.' And he left them, and getting into the boat again, he went across to the other side" (Mk 8:11–13).

The perverse and willfully blind will not be persuaded by signs. Yet the whole of Mark's Gospel is constructed as one great parable or sign, and signs are all around, in people and events, in encounters and theophanies, and in everything Jesus does and says. The coda to the gospel reiterates the message: "The Lord worked with them and confirmed the message by the signs that accompanied it" (Mk 16:20). John's Gospel further attests to the persuasiveness of the signs of Jesus (Jn 2:23; 6:2; 10:37–38).

This book has been about signs. Their interpretation is the responsibility of each and all of us.

————

If living well were like riding a bicycle, we might expect to have learnt the art by a certain age. With luck, we would never forget it. But life is more like a path in the woods, with unforeseeable twists and turns. Every life unfolds in its own unique way, and each of us is only one of the players that affects its outcome. In the course of a single lifetime, the scene can change and people find themselves in unfamiliar territory. Bike-riding is probably much easier.

Jesus said, "Ask, and you will receive; search, and you will find; knock, and the door will be opened for you" (Mt 7:7). People everywhere search for meaning, and some become reasonably content with their inquiring lives. There are those who undertake a private and individual quest, and others who learn wisdom from wise people, from cultural or religious traditions, or from the world in which they live. A few, in the spirit of Jesus, set themselves to seek, to ask, and to knock purposefully.

In these pages we have identified worlds and traditions, wisdom and folly. The range of cultures and societies demonstrates the myriad contexts in which people try to live well, whether personally, socially, or with God. Our Christian tradition takes the physical world and the multiplicity of peoples seriously, claiming that God's revelation can come to us at any time and place, through any culture, any society, and any person. Christians, therefore, have no business identifying only the bad and inferior in cultures, but must actively look for signs of God's presence.

Our lives are not static, our journeys are unending, and our conversion is never a thing of the past. Some people aspire to self-actualization, but if our lives are preoccupied with self we will never experience transcendence. The Christian is called to make a leap of faith, to get out of the boat and walk on the water, to approach ever-closer to Jesus. To fail to do this would be to fall back on our own devices, to look out for ourselves, and to turn into misers (*miser*, unhappy person, wretch). Misers are bereft of happiness. They have possessions but no relationships, they hoard rather than share, and they gather for fear of scattering. Jesus offers neither possessions nor elevated status, but the riches of peace and self-transcendence. The prize is reached only by the Way of the Cross: only when we lose our lives will we gain them (Lk 9:24). The reversals entailed by following Jesus will, however, bring life from death and peace from suffering. The Way of Jesus is neither broad nor easy, but for those who persevere by God's grace, it leads to life (Davis, 1990:41).

References
and Bibliographies

Chapter One: From Call to Response

Epigraphs:

Eboussi Boulaga: *Christianity Without Fetishes*. Maryknoll, NY: Orbis,1984: 114.

Jesse Jackson: From a speech on Martin Luther King Day, January 11, 1994.

Nathan Mitchell: *Liturgy,* Vol 1, 2. 1980.

Text:

Bynum, C.W. 1992. "Women's Stories, Women's Symbols: A Critique of Victor Turner's Theory of Liminality." In *Fragmentation and Redemption: Essays on Gender and the Human Body in Medieval Religion*. New York, NY: Zone Books.

Chittister, Joan. 1995. *The Fire in These Ashes: A Spirituality of Contemporary Religious Life*. Kansas City, MO: Sheed and Ward.

Leech, Kenneth. 1977. *Soul Friend: The Practice of Christian Spirituality.* New York, NY: Harper and Row, 1977.

Chapter Two: Ministry As Mission

Epigraphs:

Vincent Crapanzano: *Hermes' Dilemma and Hamlet's Desire: On the Epistemology of Interpretation.* Cambridge, MA: Harvard University Press, 1992:3.

Eboussi Boulaga: *Christianity Without Fetishes.* Maryknoll, NY: Orbis, 1984:68.

Leonardo Boff: *The New Evangelization: Good News to the Poor.* Maryknoll, NY: Orbis, 1990:17.

Text:

Ad Gentes [*AG*]. 1965. See *The Documents of Vatican II.*

Barrett, D. 1998. *International Bulletin of Missionary Research.* (January): 27.

Bosch, D. 1991. *Transforming Mission: Paradigm Shifts in Theology of Mission.* Maryknoll, NY: Orbis.

Burrows, W., ed. 1993. *Redemption and Dialogue: Reading* Redemptoris Missio *and* Dialogue and Proclamation. Maryknoll, NY: Orbis.

Catechism of the Catholic Church. 1994. Liguori, MO: Liguori Publications.

Crossan, J.D. 1991. *The Historical Jesus: The Life of a Mediterranean Jewish Peasant.* San Francisco, CA: Harper SanFrancisco.

Dialogue and Proclamation [*DP*]. Pontifical Council for Inter-Religious Dialogue and the Congregation for the Evangelization of Peoples. In Burrows ed. 1993: 93–118.

Documents Of Vatican II, The. 1967. London, U.K.: Geoffrey Chapman.

___ *Ad Gentes* [*AG*], *Decree on the Missionary Activity of the Church*: 584–630.

___ *Lumen Gentium* [*LG*], *Dogmatic Constitution on the Church:* 14–101.

Friedan, B. 1993. *The Fountain of Age.* New York, NY: Simon and Schuster.

Jenkinson, W. and H. O'Sullivan, eds. 1989. *Trends in Mission Theology.* Maryknoll, NY: Orbis: 399–414.

Hollenweger, W. 1979. "Evangelization in the World Today." *Concilium*, 114. New York, NY: Seabury:40–41.

Lumen Gentium [*LG*]. 1964. See *Documents of Vatican II, The*

Malina, B. 1981. *The New Testament World: Insights From Cultural Anthropology.* Atlanta, GA: John Knox.

Malina, B. 1986. *Christian Origins and Cultural Anthropology.* Atlanta, GA: John Knox.

Malina, B. 1992. *Social-Science Commentary on the Synoptic Gospels.* Minneapolis, MN: Fortress.

Meier, J. 1994. *A Marginal Jew: Rethinking the Historical Jesus.* (2 vols) New York, NY: Doubleday.

Neyrey, J. 1991. *The Social World of Luke-Acts.* Peabody, MA: Hendrickson.

Nolan, A. 1992. *Jesus Before Christianity.* Maryknoll, NY: Orbis.

Redemptoris Missio [*RM*]. 1990. An encyclical letter on the Permanent Validity of the Church's Missionary Mandate. John Paul II. In Burrows, ed.,1993:3–55.

SEDOS Seminar. 1981. See Jenkinson and O'Sullivan, eds., 1989.

Weakland, R. 1997. "United in Ministry: Exploring Common Ground." *Salesianum,* Winter: 8–16.

Chapter Three:
Stories, Parables, and Pastoral Ministry

Epigraphs:

Brain Swimme and Thomas Berry: *The Universe Story: From the Primordial Flaring Forth to the Ecozoic Era.* New York, NY: HarperSanFrancisco, 1992:3.

Fyodor Dostoevsky: *The Brothers Karamazov.*

Henry Chadwick: Review of Wayne T. Meeks, *The Origins of Christian Morality.* In *Times Literary Supplement,* August 12, 1994:28.

Text:

Chatwin, B. 1987. *The Songlines.* New York, NY: Viking.

Donnelly, D. 1992. "Pilgrims and Tourists." *Spirituality Today,* 44:23–31.

Donovan, V. 1978. *Christianity Rediscovered: An Epistle From the Maasai.* Maryknoll, NY: Orbis.

Gittins, A. 1987. "Communities of Concern." *Spirituality Today*, 39:317–330.

Sansom, B. 1982. "The Sick Who Do Not Speak." In *Semantic Anthropology*. D. Parkin, ed. London, U.K.: Academic Press, 183–195.

Wiesel, E. 1982. *The Gates of the Forest*. New York, NY: Schocken Books.

Chapter Four:
Healing and Wholeness: A Cross-Cultural Perspective

Epigraphs:

Hasidic Wisdom: in McGuiness, J. *Journey Into Compassion*. New York, Orbis: 1993:81.

Ladislas Orsy: "Dominion or Communion." *America* 169, 16 (November 20) 1993: 12.

G.K. Chesterton: *"Hymn for the Church Militant."*

Text:

Harrison, B. 1981. "The Power of Anger in the Work of Love." *Union Seminary Quarterly Review*, 36 (Supplementary): 41–57.

Katz, R. 1976. "Education for Transcendence: !Kia-Healing with the Kalahari !Kung." In Lee and DeVore, eds. *Kalahari Hunter-Gatherers*. Cambridge, MA: Harvard University Press, 1982:282–301. [The phonetic /!/ represents a click-sound]

Katz, R. 1982. *Boiling Energy: Community Healing Among the Kalahari Kung*. Cambridge, MA: Harvard University Press.

McGuiness, J. 1993. *Journey Into Compassion.* Maryknoll, NY: Orbis.

Chapter Five:
Caring and Prophecy: Retrieving a Tradition

Epigraphs:
Joan Chittister: *The Fire in These Ashes.* Kansas City, MO: Sheed and Ward. 1995:26.

Yushi Nomura: *Desert Wisdom.* New York, NY: Doubleday/ Dell, 1982.

Joan Chittister: From a talk at a *Call to Action* meeting, 1995.

Text:
Arbuckle, G. 1993. *Refounding the Church: Dissent for Leadership.* Maryknoll, NY: Orbis.

Crowe, F. 1989. "Son of God, Holy Spirit, and World Religions": 324–343. In *Appropriating the Lonergan Idea* [Chapter 19]. Michael Vertin, ed. Washington, DC: Catholic University of America Press.

Foucault, M. 1986. *The Care of the Self.* New York, NY: Pantheon Books.

Metzger, B. and M. Coogan, eds. 1993. *The Oxford Companion to the Bible.* New York, NY: Oxford University Press.

Miles, M. 1990. *Practicing Christianity: Critical Perspectives for an Embodied Spirituality.* New York, NY: Crossroad.

Nolan, A. 1992. *Jesus Before Christianity.* Maryknoll, NY: Orbis.

Quasten, J. ed. 1948. *Ancient Christian Writers [The Letter to Diognetus]*, 6. Westminster, MD: Newman Press.

Rosenblatt, M. E. 1989. "Jesus As Healer." *The Bible Today* (Jan), 10–20.

Sontag, S. [1978] 1989. "Illness As Metaphor" and "AIDS and Its Metaphors." New York, NY: Anchor Books.

Stuhlmueller, C. 1989. "Sickness and Disease: An Old Testament Perspective." *The Bible Today* (Jan), 5–9,33.

Chapter Six: Embodied Spirituality

Epigraphs:

Simone Weil: *Waiting on God.* Glasgow, U.K.: Collins, 1950:90.

Thomas Moore: *Care of the Soul,* New York, NY: Harper Collins, 1992:203.

Margaret Miles: *Practicing Christianity: Critical Perspectives for an Embodied Spirituality.* New York, NY: Crossroad, 1990:85.

Text:

Cassidy, S. 1993. *Sharing the Darkness: The Spirituality of Caring.* Maryknoll, NY: Orbis.

Csordas, T. ed. 1994. *Embodiment and Experience.* New York, NY: Cambridge University Press.

Douglas, M. 1970. *Natural Symbols.* Harmondsworth, U.K.: Penguin Books.

Harrison, B. 1981. "The Power of Anger in the Work of Love." *Union Seminary Quarterly Review, 36* (Supplementary):36:41–57.

Hastrup, K. 1993. "Hunger and the Hardness of Facts." *Man*:727–739.

Jackson, M. 1983. "Knowledge of the Body." *Man*:327–345.

McFague, S. 1993. *The Body of God: An Ecological Theology.* Minneapolis, MN.: Fortress.

Miles, M. 1990. *Practicing Christianity: Critical Perspectives for an Embodied Spirituality.* New York, NY: Crossroad.

Chapter Seven: *Growing in Age and Wisdom*

Epigraphs:

Carl Gustav Jung: Quoted in Friedan, B. *The Fountain of Age.* New York, NY: Simon and Schuster, 1993:463.

Mohammed: Quoted in Lane-Poole, S. *Speeches and Table-Talk of the Prophet Muhammad.* Asian Book Co., 1979.

Carolyn Walker Bynum: *Fragmentation and Redemption: Essays on Gender and the Human Body in Medieval Religion.* New York, NY: Zone Books, 1992:48.

Text:

Bynum, C. 1982. *Jesus As Mother: Studies in the Spirituality of the High Middle Ages.* Berkeley and Los Angeles, CA: University of California Press.

Bynum, C. 1987. *Holy Feast and Holy Fast: The Religious Significance of Food to Medieval Women.* Berkeley and Los Angeles, CA: University of California Press.

Bynum, C. 1992. *Fragmentation and Redemption: Essays on Gender and the Human Body in Medieval Religion.* New York, NY: Zone Books.

Friedan, B. 1993. *The Fountain of Age.* New York, NY: Simon and Schuster.

Gittins, A. 1998 [1989]. *Gifts and Strangers: Meeting the Challenge of Inculturation.* Mahwah, NJ: Paulist.

Gould, R. 1987. *Transformation: Growth and Change in Adult Life.* New York, NY: Simon and Schuster.

Kollar, N. 1990. "Toward a Spirituality of Pain." *Spirituality Today,* 42: 209–216.

Marty, M. 1994. "The Tradition of the Church in Health and Healing." *International Review of Mission,* (April) 227–245.

Miles, M. 1989. *Carnal Knowing: Female Nakedness and Religious Meaning in the Christian West.* Boston, MA: Beacon Press.

Nolan, A. 1992. *Jesus Before Christianity.* Maryknoll, NY: Orbis.

Nuland, S. 1993. *How We Die.* New York, NY: Vintage Books.

Quasten, J., ed. 1948. *Ancient Christian Writers [Letter to Diognetus],* 6. Westminster, MD: Newman Press.

Sontag, S. 1989. "Illness As Metaphor" and "AIDS and Its Metaphors." New York, NY: Anchor Books.

Steinberg, L. 1984. *The Sexuality of Christ in Renaissance Painting and Its Modern Oblivion.* New York, NY: Pantheon Books.

Westley, R. 1994. "We Are Makers of Love." *Praying,* (May-June).

Afterword

Davis, C. 1990. *A Spirituality for the Vulnerable.* Kansas City, MO: Sheed and Ward.

Index

About the Author

Anthony J. Gittins, CSSp, is a religious of the Congregation of the Holy Ghost (CSSp), and a member of the Volunteer Missionary Movement (VMM). A native of Manchester, England, he has taught in Chicago for fifteen years and is currently the Bishop Francis X. Ford M.M. Professor of Missiology at the Catholic Theological Union. His ministry has taken him from the villages of West Africa to the streets of Chicago. He is the author of several books, including *Bread for the Journey: The Mission of Transformation and the Transformation of Mission* (Orbis, 1993) and *Gifts and Strangers: Meeting the Challenge of Inculturation* (Paulist, 1998). A missionary, public speaker, and an active retreat leader.

This book—*Reading the Clouds: Mission Spirituality for New Times*—and its author are the recipients of the Louis G. Miller Award, sponsored by Liguori Publications in honor of Louis G. Miller, long-time editor of *Liguorian* magazine (1961–1976) and pioneer of Catholic publishing.